## Praise for *Deadly and Slick*

'A fascinating, well-researched read. Balani not only throws a retrospective spotlight on the mercurial fluidity of race, gender, class, sexuality and culture in the colonial project, she digs into the crevices to expose every lethal outcome'

Stella Dadzie, author of *A Kick in the Belly*

'An essential and lucid analysis of the long-standing but changing relationship between sexuality and race. A must read'

Maya Goodfellow, author of *Hostile Environment*

'*Deadly and Slick* is a coruscating history of marriage, empire, race-craft, the capitalist family, and the rise of "affective individualism", distilling the very best of contemporary anti-colonial, queer and Marxist theorizing, while weaving together stories about "inchoate fascists" ranging from Lord Kitchener to Priti Patel, and from Raj-era memsahibs to QAnon. Sita Balani has distilled complex ideas about the Möbius strip of race and sex into clear and pleasurable prose that takes the reader on a grim tour of the taxonomical imagination in colonial societies, all the way from Carl Linnaeus to Jordan Peterson, with important albeit discomfiting conclusions for contemporary feminist politics'

Sophie Lewis, author of *Abolish the Family* and *Full Surrogacy Now*

'Smart, lucid and funny – and so urgently needed. How can we understand how the powerful mobilise our desires and affinities in ways that deplete all our lives? What is it about the intersection of race and sexuality that remains so very hot (in all ways)? Reading Balani will help you understand why we want the things we want, and also how we can start to see what we really need'

Gargi Bhattacharyya, author of *Rethinking Racial Capitalism*

'*Deadly and Slick* is admirably nimble in navigating social and historical moving parts, all the while unfolding a compelling and coherent view of how racialisation has clung to the 'common sense' in contemporary Britain. Balani does the difficult and sometimes unglamorous intellectual work of wading through the rubble of the everyday and is rewarded with an original explosion and synthesis of high concepts. The book's excavation of subjectivity shuns pat psychologisation; its structural analysis moves beyond the stale and inert. Exciting reading for anyone who has been seeking new tools for understanding some of the enduring ugliness of "sexual modernity"'

Amber Husain, author of *Replace Me* and *Meat Love: An Ideology of the Flesh*

# Deadly and Slick

Sita Balani is a Lecturer in English at Queen Mary University of London. She is the co-author of *Empire's Endgame*. She has published in *Vice*, *Tribune*, the *White Review*, *Novara*, *Salvage*, *Ceasefire*, *Five Dials*, *Wasafiri*, and *openDemocracy*. She has appeared on BBC 3 and Novara Media and is a regular speaker at events on anti-racism, feminism, education, sexuality, and colonial history.

# Deadly and Slick

Sexual Modernity and the Making of Race

Sita Balani

**VERSO**
London • New York

First published by Verso 2023
© Sita Balani 2023
Some of the material in this book was first published, in a different form,
in 'Anxious Asian Men: "Coming Out" into Neoliberal Masculinity'
in the *Journal of Postcolonial Writing* (2019), and 'From Botany to
Community: A Legacy of Classification' in *Theatrum Botanicum*,
edited by Uriel Urlow and Shela Sheikh (Sternberg Press, 2018)

1 3 5 7 9 10 8 6 4 2

**Verso**
UK: 6 Meard Street, London W1F 0EG
US: 388 Atlantic Avenue, Brooklyn, NY 11217
versobooks.com

Verso is the imprint of New Left Books

ISBN-13: 978-1-83976-102-7
ISBN-13: 978-1-83976-103-4 (UK EBK)
ISBN-13: 978-1-83976-104-1 (US EBK)

**British Library Cataloguing in Publication Data**
A catalogue record for this book is available from the British Library

**Library of Congress Cataloging-in-Publication Data**
A catalog record for this book is available from the Library of Congress

Typeset in Minion by Biblichor Ltd, Scotland
Printed and bound by CPI Group (UK) Ltd, Croydon, CR0 4YY

# Contents

# Introduction

## Racial Regimes

*We don't cross borders, borders cross us.*

Cross-Border Collective

In *Forgeries of Memory and Meaning*, Cedric Robinson observes, 'race is mercurial – deadly and slick'.[1] That race is deadly is easy to see – we see it in the deaths of migrants trying to cross the Mediterranean; we see it in ongoing health disparities and mortality rates; we see it in the overrepresentation of racialised people in the criminal justice system. Ruth Wilson Gilmore's definition of racism as 'the state-sanctioned and/or extralegal production and exploitation of group-differentiated vulnerability to premature death'[2] is particularly useful in establishing that racism is not a simple matter of prejudice or discrimination, but a question of who has access to the means of life and who is denied them. Indeed, personal prejudice is not even a necessary component. As we shall see, laws, policies, and practices that make no mention of race nonetheless produce racial outcomes. I follow Gilmore's insistence that racial hierarchies are sanctioned by the state – sometimes the direct result of government policy and at other times the result of processes of capital accumulation or exploitation that the state upholds through wilful neglect or studied inaction. But I also emphasise that statecraft has an uneven and improvisatory quality, with many unintended consequences. I seek to trace the different forms of statecraft employed by Britain as a colonial power and as a nation-state, paying close attention to both the continuities and the points of divergence between these different iterations of modern power.

The racial taxonomy of the state – whether colonial or national – is not static or fixed but adapts to the historical circumstances. To give an example, in 1940 someone born in Bengal might have been classified by the British colonial state as a member of a 'Criminal Tribe', based on the Criminal Tribes Act, legislation first passed in 1871 and subsequently revised several times. As a result of this designation, backed by spurious ethnographic evidence, they could have been forced to report to the police every week, quarantined in a penal colony, or separated from their parents at birth. In their subjection to the British state's counterinsurgency architecture – its structures of surveillance, incarceration, and cruelty, justified simply by (assumed) ancestry – this person would have had more in common with a member of the criminalised underclass in the metropole or an indigenous person in the Americas than with a Brahmin native of British India. Just as in the metropole, criminality was viewed as an innate, hereditary quality, evidenced in part by being a sexual or gender deviant, unable or unwilling to organise one's attachments into the respectable structure of the conjugal family. Hijras, sex workers, itinerants, vagabonds, or nomadic people were viewed as criminal in both periphery and metropole. Essentially, involvement in economic activity, particularly social reproduction (the work that sustains life) which appeared to evade power's grasp – and that couldn't be harnessed for profit – made one the target of discipline, differentiation, and exclusion.

During Partition, if this person was a Muslim, they could have found themselves forced to migrate from one part of Bengal to another to reside in the newly created East Pakistan. If they were a Hindu, they may have undertaken the same perilous journey in reverse. At this point, they would be a citizen of Pakistan but still a British subject with, as Ian Sanjay Patel notes, the same right to enter and live in Britain as Winston Churchill.[3] Yet if they moved to Britain in 1960, perhaps to work in a Lancashire mill, a job for which South Asians were preferentially recruited, they might have found themselves seen as an immigrant, an interloper, despite their legal status. If they stayed in Britain, however, the social designation of foreigner might have received in favour of being identified as 'British Asian'. Perhaps, on occasion, they would still also be called a 'Paki' in the street and later struggle to find employment outside of the nighttime economy in the aftermath of deindustrialisation. In the twenty-first century, however, this would have changed again, with their faith and identity placing them within the new racial category of 'Muslim'. Perhaps they or their children might be racially profiled by counterterrorism police as a result. Finally, if they were to return to their hometown, they would find it in Bangladesh rather than in the country of East Pakistan, from which they had set off for the old colonial metropole.

As we can see, though this imaginary person stays the same, the way they are classified changes. Yet the question remains, in the face of such seemingly arbitrary and capricious operations of power: why do ordinary people often (though, crucially, not always) come to view themselves and each other through the prism of race? If 'race' is the outcome of specific processes – things that can be named, tracked down, understood, contested – how then does race retain its sense of authenticity? How can we account for the way it seems to come from the bodies of individuals rather than derive from systems of governance? Why, after so many attempts to reveal it as an elaborate construction, does it continue to appear as empirical fact? While it is clear that racism serves the interests of powerful actors – of capital in search of cheap labour, of nationalist projects dependent on racialised scapegoats – the question of how and why ordinary people continue to view themselves and each other through the prism of race requires our sustained investigation and attention. What is it that gives race its 'slickness'? What endows it with what Toni Morrison referred to as a 'lethal cling'?[4]

Robinson refers to these 'constructed social systems in which race is proposed as a justification for the relations of power' as racial regimes.[5] I take up this term here to signal that we cannot examine race in isolation but must consider it within specific social relations, with their attendant mythologies, habits, and arrangements. I suggest that the trickery of race – the way its categories have the cast of common sense, the difficulty we have in halting its production – comes down to the way in which it is embedded in everyday life through the domain we take to be most natural and essential: sexuality. The ascription of sexual differences and policies around sexual practices are pivotal to racialisation; the symbolic and social salience of sex, gender, and sexuality offers a way to make 'race' seem like common sense.

To be clear, I am not suggesting that all forms of categorisation take this form. Setting aside the relatively minor debate over 'trans-racial' identity, what makes race a distinct classification is in the assumption that it is hereditary. While one can gain a nationality or convert to a religion, race is assumed to be immutable. It is this quality that ties it inextricably to the sexual, to reproduction, gender, and kinship. In this regard, though race remains a dominant mode of categorisation, its salience is under constant revision. In the second part of the book, I consider the ways in which both racial categories and the structures of social reproduction on which they depend in modern life are both under tremendous pressure as capitalist crises intensify. This pressure is already making space for insurgent nationalist and religious formations to capture reactionary multiracial formations. While we must fight for a future without race, we must also attend to the disturbing ascendance of other violent forms of dividing the world.

Racial taxonomies depend on the management of populations – what Michel Foucault refers to as biopolitics. The modern state (whether colonial or national) employs methods of exclusion (such as deportation and incarceration) even as it distributes resources (such as healthcare and education). While it may be tempting to view the state as Janus-faced or two-sided, giving with one hand while taking with the other, these functions are less two sides of the same coin and more a continuum of measures through which populations can be managed. As Foucault observes, 'The specificity of modern racism, or what gives it its specificity, is not bound up with mentalities, ideologies, or the lies of power. It is bound up with the technique of power, with the technology of power'.[6] To theorise this connection between population management and the making of racial categories, David Theo Goldberg uses the term 'the racial state'. He observes that states are racial not because they produce racialised outcomes but because of their role in 'population definition, determination, and structuration'.[7] Techniques to manage the broad domain of social reproduction – sex, domestic life, the family unit, children – are difficult to distinguish from the management of race, because it is through the management of social reproduction that race is made and maintained at the level of both social structures and common sense.

The governing rationale used to legitimise this biopolitical form of state power is nationalism: we are led to believe that the population over which a state rules is an organic community which precedes any attempt to manage it. Though no nation-state has ever come into being in this way, the myth of an organic national polity continues to animate racial logic. This umbilical connection from race to nationalism makes visible the work needed to maintain the salience of race. As Radhika Mongia observes, 'a blurring of the vocabularies of nationality and race is a founding strategy of the modern (nation) state'.[8] The naturalisation of the nation-state system as a means of global organisation makes nationalism appear benign, advancing the claim that each of us belongs to a nation-state to which we must show loyalty and by which we will be protected.

This putative universalism offers defensive cover for the racial ideologies advanced by nationalist projects, while licensing the forms of statecraft needed to maintain racial regimes. From welfare projects to war, the nation-state promises to act for the benefit of its citizens, but this promise is dependent on exclusion. As Gargi Bhattacharyya puts it, 'Citizenship takes its meaning from the implication that there is an outside, a space of non-citizenship where such rights and entitlements do not apply'.[9] Outsiders – whether internal or external to the nation – are used to define who is included. According to Etienne Balibar, racism is a 'supplement internal to nationalism, always in excess of it, but always indispensable to its constitution'.[10] Nationalism can rarely stake its claims without recourse to the metaphors of kinship: citizens are encouraged to view one another as family, to view political leaders as standing *in loco parentis*; and to view their own intimate relations as a model for citizenship. In this way, the nation-state acts as the formal structure through which the categories of sexuality and gender are maintained as the guarantor of racial difference.

## Sexuality and Culture

*The racial was always cultural, the essential never unequivocal.*

Robert Young

In this book, I argue that race is made under the conditions of sexual modernity. By 'sexual modernity' I mean the arrangement of sexual life, gender, and kinship through which capitalist social relations are secured. As capitalism incorporated, transformed, or destroyed other ways of life and their attendant sex, gender, and kinship arrangements, companionate marriage, nuclear families, and a binary gender system took hold. This shift came with the promise that one can find meaning, comfort, and care in romantic love and familial intimacy. But sexual life is not contained by these institutions of respectability: other forms of sex, whether consensual or exploitative, are just as ubiquitous, even if denied or obscured in official accounts. Racial Others are measured in their distance from these respectable forms of kinship. Further, illicit sexual practices are intertwined with the making of race. Sexual violence is used as a tool of racial terror to discipline subject populations, expropriate land, or control the movement of people.

Race, gender, and sexuality, then, are inextricable from each other. In the current moment, 'intersectionality' has become a prominent way to understand how the categories of race, gender, and sexuality interact. Though the concept originates in Black feminist scholarship,[11] it now circulates unmoored from its original object of critique, incorporated into the rhetoric of vague liberal inclusivity. Even corporate diversity and inclusion training now promises an 'intersectional' approach, and where racialised people were once erroneously referred to as 'diverse', they are now erroneously described as 'intersectional'. Though intersectionality has proven useful in addressing discrimination claims within the legal context that the term originally sought to address, it has little explanatory power as to how these categories are constructed and maintained. In other words, in order to view race and gender as identity categories that intersect in a single person, one has to consider race as already separate from gender. In doing so, one obscures the way in which these categories were never pure or separate. Race was always intertwined with the messy work of sexuality; the sexed body and its gendered implications took shape through racial science.

Extending Paul Gilroy's suggestion that 'gender is the modality in which race is lived',[12] I suggest that gender and sexuality do not 'intersect' with race as correspondent categories so much as form the discursive, legislative, and experiential material of race. In part I of the book, I'll trace the historical emergence of these categories – of race, gender, and sexuality – in order to explore, in part II, the ways in which they are maintained and finessed – and sometimes break down – in contemporary Britain. It is common to suggest that colonial science constructed racial categories as biological realities and that the 'New Racism' of the postwar period rejected biological racism while conserving race under the sign of culture.[13] In this narrative, culture supersedes biology and comes to function as a codeword for race. Though this story is highly compelling, its teleology is too simple. Culture has always functioned as the alibi for race, not because it offers a more polite language for domination but because it offers a more compelling story. Under colonial rule, appeals to biology were always also appeals to culture. As nation-states became the fundamental unit of geopolitical organisation, appeals to culture – to the imagined shared traditions, customs, and values of a people with a primordial attachment to a particular territory, usually understood to constitute a racial group – served as the rationalising logic for national governments.

While writers have noted how racial conflicts in Britain express themselves through the language of culture, the role of sexuality and gender in these conflicts has been relegated to a subdomain and remained under-theorised as a result. Borrowing from Rahul Rao's reading of B. R. Ambedkar, I suggest that we might think of culture (the premiere alibi for race) and sexuality as fundamentally inseparable. According to Ambedkar, the prohibition on intermarriage is not simply a technique of the caste system but is essential to its function. As such, gender does not intersect with caste, it *becomes* caste through endogamy. Caste does not intersect with gender but actively shapes gendered subjects.[14] We might see culture and sexuality in a similar fashion. We see traces of this indivisibility in everyday life: when someone wants to decry or defend a particular gendered or sexual practice (such as veiling), they inevitably described it as 'cultural'. In doing so, they betray the ways in which the organisation of kinship, sexual life, and gender are viewed as the foundational distinctions between 'cultures' – they are mobilised as that which gives 'race' its meaning.

This is no mere rhetorical flourish; organising people into distinct groups (with attendant and fixed cultures) and calcifying or attempting to transfer their sexual, gender, and kinship arrangement was the hallmark of colonial governance. As Edward Said notes, rather than simply characterise colonised people as subhuman, colonial authorities enlivened the relationship between ruler and ruled by stressing 'the fact that the Oriental lived in a different but thoroughly organized world of his own, a world with its own national, cultural, and epistemological boundaries and principles of internal coherence'.[15] Nicholas Dirks describes the operation of this logic in British India: colonial authorities constructed an 'ethnographic state' that was 'driven by the belief that India could be ruled using anthropological knowledge to understand and control its subjects, and to represent and legitimate its own mission'.[16] Matters of sexuality were the cornerstones of the ethnographic knowledge produced for this purpose, with manuals detailing kinship practices and marriage rituals distributed as guides for the colonial police force, army recruiters, revenue agents, and district magistrates.

Trying to stabilise British rule on the subcontinent, colonial authorities attempted to catalogue native sexual mores under the heading of tradition. As Dirks notes, 'Cultural forms in societies newly classified as "traditional" were reconstructed and transformed by this knowledge, which created new categories and oppositions between colonizers and colonized, European and Asian, modern and traditional, West and East'.[17] The sexuality of subject people, even if viewed as deviant, violent, and dangerous, was nonetheless understood to have its own clear rationale – distinct from the West, and inferior to it, but justified by cultural particularity. As such, we can see culture and sexuality not as two separate analytic realms that sometimes cross but as a Möbius strip, in some moments operating as two sides of the same entity and at others turning into one another. I borrow this image from Rahul Rao, who observes that 'rather like a Möbius strip, caste is the regulation of gender, which is caste'.[18] Like watching a Möbius strip turning, there is something both mesmerising and unsettling about this process, it has a hypnotic quality that can both provoke and prevent analysis. In this book, I'll try to follow the Möbius strip as it twists and folds back on itself.

## British Asians

*Studies of Asian communities pored endlessly over the fascinating cultural features of arranged marriages, kinship systems and religious rituals.*

Claire Alexander

In the chapters that follow, I attempt to show how sexual modernity underpins modern racial regimes. For several reasons, I focus my attention on British Asians. The slippery, contradictory, and volatile work of racialisation becomes particularly visible when we examine a specific group, tracking the different ways in which they are classified, understood, and managed over time. Further, in a group highly stratified by class and divided by religion, we can see the work race does to both cohere and divide. Though I use the term 'British Asian' as shorthand, I am aware that it is highly insufficient, carrying with it the trace of a particular historical moment in the late twentieth century in which 'hyphenated' identities were in vogue and some rather banal questions of culture, diaspora, and national belonging were part of popular discourse. My own coming-of-age in this period is no doubt one of the reasons I continue to use this term. Here, though, I hope it can stand in for a more general concern with the interactions between the British state (in both colonial and national iterations) and the various peoples who can trace their roots to the South Asian subcontinent.

An examination of British Asians helps to mine Said's observation that Orientalism works through paradox. South Asians in Britain are cast simultaneously as docile, perhaps assimilable, *and* as incorrigibly attached to their cultural difference, as potential model minorities *and* as a potential terrorist threat. In contemporary Britain, Hindus and Sikhs are understood to embody assimilation, while Muslims are viewed as a threat, though at earlier moments in the postwar period, religious distinctions were less prominent. This bifurcated logic has its origins in the particular position of the Indian subcontinent in the British Empire. Coined by Benjamin Disraeli as 'the brightest jewel in the crown', British officials often described their deep love of India, while also considering it barbaric or uncivilised. Colonial education on the subcontinent was developed as a means of creating a comprador elite – 'a class of persons Indian in blood and colour, but English in tastes, in opinions, in morals and in intellect'.[19] These ideas reappear in postcolonial governance in Britain, with 'community leaders' and culturalism deployed as a means of rerouting antiracist dissent, preventing differently racialised communities from finding common cause on the basis of shared exploitation, and maintaining the authority of the racial order.

Various techniques of colonial governance tested across the world were finessed in British India, in which the vast territory of South Asia was subject to multiple forms of governance. The system of indirect rule, conceived of by Frederick Lugard and trialled in Uganda and Nigeria, had especially potent effects in British India. Indirect rule worked from the basis that, rather than attempt to directly dominate huge populations with military force alone, native elites should be recruited to manage the unruly masses on behalf of colonial governments. Princely states, for example, covered 40 per cent of the area of pre-independence India and were governed via alliances between local or indigenous rulers and the British colonial authorities. This system helped to give the appearance of some modicum of indigenous sovereignty, while the doctrine of paramountcy ensured that British colonial authorities maintained their dominance, ensuring the smooth operation of resource extraction. This method of control helped to reinforce the notion that British rule was a benevolent, collaborative process which operated according to respect for native custom. As Mahmood Mamdani wryly observes, 'Britain, more than any other power, keenly glimpsed the authoritarian possibilities in culture'.[20] In this obsession with culture, tradition, and the cultivation of a native elite, British control of the subcontinent calcified and exploited the pre-existing divisions of caste and religion. These distinctions reappear in postcolonial governance, with Hindus and Sikhs viewed as closer to inhabiting sexual modernity than their Muslim counterparts.

Furthermore, under the guise of respect for cultural difference and concern about 'barbaric' cultural practices, colonial social legislation focussed heavily on issues of sexuality. By codifying – and sometimes legislating – sexual practices and the family form, the colonial state was able to make radical changes to land relations, for example by aligning zamindars (landowners) with bourgeois kinship structures for the purposes of expropriation and exploitation. Examining these histories allows us to understand more fully the ways in which sexual modernity has long produced and maintained the racial order. It also helps us to grasp the ways in which ideas about deviant or debased sexual practices are used to racialise South Asians at the border, in the education system, and in wider regimes of representation.

By tracing the interactions between South Asians and the biopolitical apparatus, both in the imperial context and in the metropole, I hope to illuminate the ways in which the colonial context functioned as a laboratory for techniques of government that would later be used on the British mainland. This is not to say that national governance is simply a continuation of empire. Rather, in examining continuity as well as change, we can gain a clearer understanding of the distinct predicaments of modernity. Though I take British Asians as a case study, I contend that the imbrication of sexual modernity with the making of race can be traced across different imperial and national contexts, albeit with different idioms, consequences, and iconic

modes of sexual deviance in each. Further, though race has transnational dimensions, it is not always the operative form of division.
As such, this book does not attempt to account for the racial politics
of contemporary South Asia, nor of the dynamics of caste and religion
in that context.

Part 1 explores key developments in the making of sexual modernity. In the first chapter, I set out the distinctive historical features
of sexual modernity, showing the limits of a Foucauldian analysis
which obscures gender and the colonies and, in doing so, is unable
to grasp the fundamental imbrication of sexuality and race. In
chapter 2, I consider how colonial science, especially botany and
zoology, produced 'races' as discrete types in its schema of human
variation. By returning to this history to reveal the generative power
of sexuality, I set up the epistemological context for colonial rule.
In chapter 3, I consider the figure that stands at the apex of colonial
sexual modernity – the white bourgeois man – to show the ways in
which his position both produces and subordinates wayward or
unruly sexual subjects, such as sex workers. In chapter 4, I consider
the use of the family in the contraction of free movement and the
expansion of the welfare state – twinned processes of national
statecraft through which some could be made deserving, respectable
citizens and others could be excluded from the promise of sexual
modernity.

In part II of the book, I turn my attention more squarely to
contemporary Britain, to show how sexual modernity reaches its apex
at the turn of the twenty-first century, with sexual freedom now
treated as the ultimate mode of individuality. Political and economic
conflicts have been recoded as issues of national identity, in which
sexual freedom is a sign of progressive, modern Britain, threatened
by oppressive and alien sexual values held by intransigent minorities.
In this context, the ability to develop one's own sexuality is assumed
to be at the core of the authentic self: the freedom to pursue sexual
desires, romantic love, marriage, and the nuclear family marks us as
discrete individuals. I work from the premise that in the early years
of the twenty-first century, self-realisation is conceived of as a responsibility rather than as a possibility. Willingness to conform to the

rules of the sexual market is understood to make one a good citizen, ready for the labour market.

The politics of sexuality are continually renewed in contemporary Britain, as culture and policy respond to the everyday reality of a multicultural society. As racial taxonomies have been organised around sexual difference, race in contemporary life is given salience through questions of gender, sexuality, and kinship. In the twenty-first century, regressive and dangerous sexual proclivities are ascribed to Muslims, while Hindus and Sikhs are viewed as ripe for assimilation into sexual modernity. Through this Islamicisation of older racial logics, Muslim communities are assumed to exist in opposition to sexual freedom, tied to restrictive traditions, cultures, and beliefs. This view informed the operations of the 'War on Terror', functioning as the implicit logic behind sexual torture, for example. Sexual restriction thus operates as a kind of sexual difference, one that risks perverting a broader culture wherein the sexual freedom of the individual subject is sacred.

As the hold of monogamy and the nuclear family weakens, however, sexual experimentation and individual gender expression have become more prominent aspects of sexual modernity, seen as increasingly central to individual self-realisation. Though greater numbers are experimenting with non-monogamy and embracing gender identities outside of the man/woman binary, sexual violence and exploitation remain an ordinary facet of everyday life. While the couple form may be losing some of its lustre, social reproduction remains heavily privatised, with dwindling state support placing heavier burdens on individuals to care for themselves. Further, transphobia has become a powerful reactionary flashpoint, with multiracial and transnational coalitions forming in defence of the sexual dyad. These formations are often tied to anti-migrant xenologies, conspiracy theories, and moral panics regarding the sexual abuse of children.

To begin part II, I show how Britain's New Labour government attempted to harness the narrative of sexual freedom, particularly through their embrace of gay rights, so as to appear progressive and modern on social issues while enacting new and brutal forms of punishment to those seen to inhabit sexual modernity's underbelly. In chapter 6, I explore the ways in which Muslim men are viewed as 'trapped between cultures' – between the promise of sexual modernity and the constraints of tradition. Within the lurid imaginary of the War on Terror, they emerge as violent, abject, and terroristic folk devils who lurk in the shadows of sexual modernity and require surveillance, incarceration, and banishment.

In the final two chapters of the book, I consider the ways in which the promise of sexual modernity is fracturing. Its claim that family, romantic love, and individual sexual freedom might offer some protection from the impersonal and volatile demands of capitalism can no longer hold. While new kinds of freedom are being constructed in the cracks and from the fragments, this rupture does not herald the end of race but a reorganisation of racial regimes and a resurgence of authoritarian nationalism. In chapter 7, I explore the peculiar and powerful work that associations between brown women and violence can do to uphold authoritarian state violence. I consider the spectacle of 'Jihadi brides' as heralding a shift from thinking of British Asian women as victims of tradition to seeing them as agents of subversion who might betray the benevolent British nation. Finally, in chapter 8, I turn to the controversy surrounding LGBT sex education to show the counterintuitive way that diversity, gay rights, and gender equality emerge as 'British Values' during a time of biting austerity and political instability. I consider the ways in which Britain's racial politics depend on a paranoid psychogeography that considers Muslim communities as harbouring powerful forms of authority that could undermine the apparently universal values of sexual modernity. Finally, I suggest that though diverse gender expression and sexual experimentation are emerging as sexual modernity's new horizons of possibility, they offer little respite from the deterioration of social and economic life.

## Interlocutors

*Can one divide human reality, as indeed human reality seems to be*
*genuinely divided, into clearly different cultures, histories, traditions,*
*societies, even races, and survive the consequences humanly?*

Edward Said

My methodological approach is grounded in British cultural studies,
particularly in the work produced by the Centre for Contemporary
Cultural Studies (CCCS) at the University of Birmingham. I am
guided by their insistence on the indivisibility of racism and
nationalism, the central role of moral panics in managing capitalist crisis, and the importance of thinking conjuncturally. In
part II, I follow this conjunctural approach, attempting to understand the ways in which economic and political crises condense in
stories of racialised sexual deviance. I am particularly influenced
by Stuart Hall's reflections on the utility of 'hegemony' to an
understanding of race and racism. In his essay 'Gramsci's Relevance
for the Study of Race and Ethnicity', Hall's Gramscian approach
yields that

> the so-called 'self' which underpins these ideological formations
> is not a unified but a contradictory subject and a social construc-
> tion. He [Gramsci] thus helps us to understand one of the most
> common, least explained features of 'racism': the 'subjection' of the
> victims of racism to the mystifications of the very racist ideologies
> which imprison and define them.[21]

This sense of the constructed, fragmented, and contradictory subject
is crucial to my understanding of how race persists despite its fictive
quality. Further, identifying the way in which victims of racism have
no immunity from racist ideology without resorting to a simple
invocation of 'false consciousness' or 'internalised racism' is essential
to understanding the role that racialised subjects play in upholding
racism both institutionally and culturally.

Gramsci also advanced the idea that common sense was not a singular view borne of a clear ideology, but the various bits and pieces of ideas – sometimes half-formed, misunderstood, and contradictory – that sediment into a shared, popular philosophy. Hall and Alan O'Shea build on this, defining common sense as 'everyday thinking that provides a framework of meaning in order to make sense of the world . . . that expresses itself in the vernacular, the familiar language of the street, the home, the pub, the workplace and the terraces'.[22] As such, in this project, I am attentive to how ideas about sexuality and race are threaded into the language of the everyday, reading closely for the ways in which the demotic expresses sedimented ideas. As Hall notes, the popular imaginary 'gets expressed in the dirty, compromised, commercialized, over-ridden world of popular culture, which is never an un-contradictory space, never an uncontested space'.[23] It is this notion that leads me to attend to television programmes and popular memoirs in chapters 5, 6 and 7. It is through the project of cultural studies – with its distinctive blend of close reading from literary studies with a rigorous and original materialism – that an analysis of race in Britain was made possible but was also by no means exhausted. It is to this intellectual tradition that I hope to contribute with this book, not least because the role of sexuality has been somewhat underemphasised in this body of work.

I am guided by queer theory's interest in the normative and the ordinary – for example, in treating marriage as an arcane ritual act through which we can discern the hegemonic force of heterosexuality. This book has been shaped by critical writing on the imbrication of mainstream gay rights and Western imperialism. Jasbir Puar's work on 'homonationalism' was highly influential to my thinking. Puar examines post-9/11 American culture to show the ways in which gay rights can be cleaved to neo-imperial projects of nation building and foreign intervention.[24] Her analysis builds on Lisa Duggan's writing on homonormativity, which observes the way in which the growing acceptance – or even embrace – of respectable homosexual life heralds neoliberalism's apex.[25]

Where my work differs from this analysis, however, is in a more stringent questioning of the term 'sexuality' itself. In this book, I try to place homonationalism – the deployment of gay rights in service to nationalism – within a longer history of imperialism and sexual modernity. I suggest that the significance of gay marriage might be that it is a revealing instance of how a social group moves from the ranks of the wayward to the civilised, from the underbelly of sexual modernity to its 'light side', able to emulate and embody its respectable habits. Queer theory has largely viewed this new inclusion as a kind of capitulation to the suffocating norms of the straight world, an abandonment of 'radical' queer politics. My own analysis, however, aligns more closely with the work of the late Christopher Chitty, who observes that gays are invited into the institutions of marriage and family at precisely the moment in which they offer little protection from the uncertainties and deprivations of late capitalism.

While queer theory has, in no small part, aided my thinking, I remain sceptical about its investments in sexual deviance as a form of – or substitution for – politics. Indeed, I am sceptical that much of what self-identified queers are up to could even be considered sexually deviant at this point. These days, queer culture is often mediated by massive multinational streaming corporations or is the subject of blockbuster art shows at galleries sponsored by oil companies. While a radical trans politics has recently begun to inaugurate a renewed queer Marxism, trans liberalism (to use Nat Raha's coinage) is following closely in the tracks of liberal lesbian and gay politics.[26] As such, my focus in this project is less on the position of self-proclaimed sexual deviants and more on the ways in which apparently heterosexual or cisgender political subjects find themselves excluded from the spoils of respectability.

In this approach, I take inspiration from Cathy Cohen's 1997 paradigm-shifting 'Punks, Bulldaggers, and Welfare Queens: The Radical Potential of Queer Politics', in which she argues that in its focus on homosexuality, queer theory, and politics hides the fact that the sexual lives of poor and racialised people are subject to precisely the policing and pathologising that class and race protects many gay people from facing.[27] It strikes me that Cohen's argument can be taken further: we need not only to look outside of LGBT lifeworlds for sexual practices that disturb or unsettle, but also begin to unravel our attachment to the idea of sexual practices as having any particular radical potential at all.

Further, while queer life and culture – and its comfortably institutional counterparts – have moved away from a critique of categories towards their veneration, this book begins from a critique of taxonomy. We live in a moment in which identity categories are understood in increasingly programmatic ways in leftist social movements. As Olúfẹ́mi O. Táíwò observes, 'The call to "listen to the most affected" or "centre the most marginalized" is ubiquitous in many academic and activist circles'. But as he goes on to explain, the 'most affected' is often conceived of in terms of identity, allowing for elite members of a particular social group to speak on behalf of those who experience much more profound marginalisation or brutality. Táíwò refers to this as 'deference epistemology' and argues that this allows for an elite class of racialised people to bolster their own careers at the expense of broader social transformations.[28] As such, though I understand why identity has taken hold as a way of understanding one's place in the world, this work is an attempt to take a step back and try to loosen our attachment to identity categories. In this fashion, I see my work in dialogue with postcolonial and planetary humanisms in which the possibility of a world without race functions as an essential political and ethical horizon.

Attempts to, in Aimé Césaire's words, construct 'a humanism made to the measure of the world' are attentive to the fatal exclusions of Enlightenment philosophy while maintaining that we cannot proceed without a sense of collective humanity. This task is most visible in Sylvia Wynter's work on the 'coloniality of being', in which she theorises the human as *homo narrans*: the shape of our being depends on the story we tell about ourselves, on our collective 'descriptive statement'. In this project, I seek to reveal how a particular model of sexuality has become a defining characteristic of 'the human', a key part of the 'descriptive statement' which is used to discipline racialised people.[29] Because of the way the logics of race are threaded into everyday life, the process of determining a new and liberatory understanding of the human is, inevitably, difficult. To move beyond the trap of sexual modernity, all aspects of the social world, of subjectivity, of being human will have to be uprooted in the process.

As you will have gathered from these opening few pages, this book takes as its focus the profoundly damaging work done by our limited conception of sexuality, the ways in which the idea of sexuality as the foundation of being becomes fatally intertwined with the making of race and the ongoing upheavals of modernity. Yet sex itself – not only the acts but the whole sphere of the erotic – is the source of a glorious, anarchic, transformative power. As a form of pleasure that is free, creative, collaborative, it could be endowed with an anti-authoritarian, anti-capitalist impulse. Many thinkers of modern selfhood – Freud, Foucault, Marcuse, Butler – have riffed on this theme. So too have all my favourite poets – Sharon Olds, Audre Lorde, Adrienne Rich, June Jordan. The singers of R&B tunes, and the painters of human figures. The ancients. This power is not the subject of this book, but it remains present nonetheless. The dispersed life force of the erotic always overspills the rigid categories that make it. Its promise for our collective liberation is so far, tragically, unfulfilled. While I cannot do justice to this potential here, my hope is that in showing how sexuality is harnessed to race-thinking, I can contribute in some small way to undermining this fatal connection.

# 1

# Sexual Modernity

## The Promise of Modern Life

*What is peculiar to modern societies, in fact, is not that they consigned
sex to a shadow existence, but that they dedicated themselves to
speaking of it ad infinitum, while exploiting it as the secret.*

Michel Foucault, *History of Sexuality, Vol. 1*

In contemporary life, sexuality is assumed to be at the heart of an
authentic self. When a baby is born, we ask what sex it is; formal
titles indicate gender and, for women, marital status; and, despite
declining marriage and rising divorce rates, for many, getting married
remains a key milestone in the narrative of an individual life. The
rise of companionate marriage in the eighteenth century opened up
the possibility for marriage to be understood as rooted in love,
companionship, and intimacy, with its economic and social imperatives increasingly obscured or denied. Marriage became the means
through which the sexual dyad could be given form and meaning as
the relationship of complementary opposites, diverging from earlier
views of woman as simply an incomplete or deformed instance of
man. Companionate marriage opens the door for romantic love to
operate as the fundamental quest for meaning. The search for a
romantic partner is now seen as a universal goal for gay and straight
people alike, and this quest is the foundational story of great swathes
of popular and high culture, from *Pride and Prejudice* to *Love Island*.
In recent years, however, the search for romantic love has come under
significant pressure, as the couple form offers increasingly paltry

protection from economic and psychic insecurity and now competes with the imperative to have varied and exciting sexual experiences and to craft a unique, authentic, expressive gender identity.

In these examples, I intentionally bring the sexed body, gender, sexual orientation, and kinship together, where others might (for good reason) seek to separate them out. I do so because in the notion of sexual freedom that guides the contemporary moral economy, these ideas work together; it is assumed that each element plays a role in an individual life. Sexual choice is articulated as a unique form of freedom: early sexual modernity, beginning in the late seventeenth century, views this choice through the lens of companionate marriage, complementary gender roles, respectable social norms, and freedom from extended family. As we'll see, racialised Others were measured and categorised by the distance between their kinship structure and this model. Contemporary sexual modernity, emerging in the twentieth century and reaching its apex in the early years of the 2000s, views sexuality as the ultimate truth of the sovereign individual; all barriers to sexual fulfilment must be removed to realise essential human freedom. Racialised Others are measured and categorised by their distance from this freedom. The overarching promise of sexual modernity has been that we can live fulfilling, happy lives through the successful pursuit of romantic love, conjugal families, sexual pleasure, and nucleated social reproduction. This promise is not a mere banality, but something tremendously powerful: the promise of love, care, self-realisation, autonomy, and meaning. In the twenty-first century, the fractures in this idea – the way in which it so regularly fails to deliver on its promise – are becoming more pronounced, and a vision of sexual freedom based on creative gender expression and sexual diversity is on the ascendancy.

Though the model of sexual freedom changes, it is continually understood to be at the heart of the individual self – a story that defines the most recent iteration of what I call 'sexual modernity'. By this, I don't simply mean the sexual elements of modernity, but that modernity is itself intertwined with sexuality. Modernity is a contradictory thing. The upheavals at the birth of capitalism inaugurated a world centred on man rather than on God; a world in which the old certainties were fractured, and from their pieces a new set of possibilities could be constructed. Europeans began to view man as separate from nature, no longer as different iterations of God's creation but instead in a position of superiority from which to divide and dominate. By harnessing the power of the natural world, man (and only man) could take control of his own destiny. The promise of modernity was found in the possibility of individual transformation, autonomy, and progress; its dangers were in the threat of disintegration, alienation, and disorientation. This web of promise and threat, danger and opportunity, thickens around questions of sexuality, gender, and kinship – in the spaces which claim to be ahistorical and intimate but are, paradoxically, the product of massive historical shifts. To understand the emergence of sexual modernity, I turn to the seminal theorist of sexuality and the self, Michel Foucault.

According to Foucault, the nineteenth century saw the idea of sexuality give an 'artificial unity' to a host of 'anatomical elements, biological functions, conducts, sensations and pleasures'.[1] The fictitious unity of sexuality 'became a causal principle, an omnipresent meaning, a secret to be discovered everywhere: sex was thus able to function as a universal signifier and as a universal signified'. In this suggestion, Foucault overturns the idea of Victorian sexual prudery to suggest that the apparent repression of sexuality also produced many more ways to discuss sexuality ('a steady proliferation of discourses') and many more injunctions to speak – to confess, deny, explain, narrate one's own sexual life.[2]

Foucault traces this process to developments in Europe, through which sex – the acts of the body's distinct erotic pleasures – was transformed into discourse. He identifies confession, medicine, education, policing, and the family as the key sites for the proliferation of sexual discourse, through which sexuality becomes understood as an essence. In the extension and intensification of confession in the seventeenth century, for example, we see the focus shift from acts to thoughts:

According to the new pastoral, sex must not be named imprudently, but its aspects, its correlations, and its effects must be

pursued down to their slenderest ramifications: a shadow in a
daydream, an image too slowly dispelled, a badly exorcised complicity between the body's mechanics and the mind's complacency:
everything had to be told.[3]

In the injunction to 'tell everything', a new political subject was
born. To borrow from Goethe's Faust (whom Marshall Berman
identifies as an archetypal modern man), this made 'space for many
millions/to live, not securely, but free for action'.[4] In other words,
modernity offered a new sense of the self – a self with agency and
autonomy – but with this freedom came the anxiety of being responsible for one's own failure, loss, and sin. This complex articulation
of freedom and insecurity has persisted at each state of sexual
modernity's evolution.

We can read this emergent subject of modernity – this subject who
must agonise over his desires, contemplate and confess his inner life,
measure his sexual imagination against a social morality – in dialogue
with the development of Christian ideas of an inner dialogue with
God. Charles Taylor notes that the eighteenth century saw the inner
dialogue with God transformed into having a dialogue with one's
own inner depths. Initially, this dialogue is simply a means to connect
with the divine, though it later becomes seen as an inherent moral
good, a marker of a complete self. As Taylor summarises,

On the original view, the inner voice is important because it tells
us what is the right thing to do. Being in touch with our moral
feelings would matter here, as a means to the end of acting rightly.
What I'm calling the displacement of the moral accent comes about
when being in touch takes on independent and crucial moral
significance. It comes to be something we have to attain to be true
and full human beings.[5]

As sexual modernity progresses, the moral accent is displaced once
again, this time onto sexuality. The notion that the 'inner voice'
speaks an 'authentic' truth, and that morality is intuitive rather than
something to be learnt or calculated, becomes articulated to a vision

of sexual conduct. This metaphysics of the self culminates in the conception of sexuality as the authentic inner truth – as 'what we really really want'.[6]

These developments to Christian practice in Europe would not have gained such an enduring purchase on collective life had they not been buttressed by marked changes in other institutions. In the eighteenth century, schools began to view children as potential sexual deviants, and the family was enlisted to conduct surveillance on young people to prevent masturbation. Psychiatry and the law conspired to categorise and discipline those who could or would not conform to the codes of sexual respectability: 'children, mad men and women, and criminals; the sensuality of those who did not like the opposite sex'.[7] In the process of naming and in the explosion of discourse, however, a set of other possibilities emerged; those who had been named as deviant could harness this label and use it as the means through which to cohere themselves, both individually and as a social group. This possibility – which Foucault names 'reverse discourse' – is most visible in the case of homosexuals. Since Foucault, the study of sexuality has largely accepted this genealogy, but in doing so it has often reproduced Foucault's own blind spots regarding the development of global capitalism and its concomitant production of gender and race.

Foucault suggests that sexuality becomes a technology of the bourgeois self that sets it apart from the aristocracy and the popular classes, acting as a measure of their fitness to rule. But this approach tends to assume that bourgeois sexual norms are simply adopted across the rest of society through their institutionalisation in the church, the family, the law, and so on, that everyone truly desires sexual respectability and seeks to emulate bourgeois codes of conduct. We might think of these developments – the emergence of bourgeois norms around the management of the self, the control of one's sexual urges, the consolidation of romantic love and the conjugal family as the unit of social, economic, and psychic life – as the promise of sexual modernity. But this promise is only half of the story.

## The Underbelly of Sexual Modernity

*It has been nine years of complicity by different levels of authority . . .*
*You mean nobody took note if indeed she was killed by a soldier in a*
*hotel and thrown into a septic tank? Did the soldier carry her to the*
*septic tank by himself?*

Irene Wangui on the murder of Agnes Wanjiru

What we are promised as modern subjects – individuality, autonomy, the freedom to pursue romantic love and sexual adventure – depends on the disavowal, sometimes even destruction, of other sexual and kinship arrangements. As Maria Lugones notes, 'Biological dimorphism, heterosexualism, and patriarchy are all characteristic of what I call the light side of the colonial/modern organization of gender'.[8] The 'light side', as Lugones puts it, does not exist in a vacuum, nor is it self-sustaining – it is dependent on all sorts of hidden or disavowed practices, often violent and exploitative, sometimes exciting and powerful, regularly crossing the lines of race and class, and rarely acknowledged as the 'other side' of sexual modernity. To give an example, while the US defended its occupation of Afghanistan in the name of women's liberation, American soldiers engaged in sexual torture in Abu Ghraib. The latter is not an exception to sexual modernity, but an essential part of how it functions. This arrangement has produced all kinds of wayward subjects – those who cannot reach or will not aspire to sexual modernity's promise of the good life, those who remain exploited by its hidden violence and the shame it lodges in its victims. In the following chapters, I'll consider the marginalised but psychically central position of sex workers and 'Eurasians' in British India, in dialogue with the highly sexualised Muslim folk devils that organise Britain's contemporary racial regime.

Where Lugones and other decolonial thinkers (such as Walter Mignolo) identify the obverse of modernity as coloniality, in order to capture the unspoken production of racial hierarchy in capitalist modernity, I find this formulation too definitive. The firm division of colony from metropole opens the door for a romanticisation of precolonial epistemologies and their attendant sex/gender systems. This division can also obscure the ways in which the promise of self-realisation through romantic love has global resonance, not because it has been violently imposed at every turn but because it resonates with people. As Rao notes with regard to the adoption of 'Western' gay norms by middle-class people in the Global South, 'homonormativity derives its power not simply from the material wherewithal of its proponents, but from its ability to shape desire by making itself synonymous with modernity, giving it mass appeal or, in a word, hegemony'.[9] If we obscure the appeal of sexual modernity's vision of the good life, a moral rather than political understanding of sexuality can take hold.

Instead, I want to suggest that the underbelly of sexual modernity comprises a huge range of sexual practices, imbricated with processes of racialisation. Struggles for more expansive forms of sexual freedom often celebrate sexual deviance as that which escapes or rebels against the limitations of sexual respectability. For example, queer theorists such as Lee Edelman and Leo Bersani offer joyful and compelling accounts of cruising – casual, public sex between men – as a distinctive and anti-establishment aspect of gay life, exciting precisely because it exists in the underbelly, disavowed by the respectable world. But we must also account for many other disavowed or denied practices, particularly for intransigent practices of violation and exploitation, such as those that attend resource extraction, militarism, and the border regime. Sexual violence is not an aberration or deviation, it plays just as significant a role in sexual modernity as the promise of self-realisation.

The path-breaking research of Marxist feminist Sylvia Federici is particularly instructive here: she observes that in the bloody and protracted early stages of capitalist development, communal lands (which could be used to sustain life for all) were enclosed and women's bodies became their substitute. 'Women themselves became the commons',[10] a site for the 'free' production of labour power to be appropriated by capital, as I'll discuss further in the next section. The rise of witch hunts in Western Europe were a key mechanism through which women's movement, labour, and power could be controlled, expropriated, and domesticated. Federici follows the grooves of colonial expansion to observe the export of witch hunts to Latin America in the seventeenth century and South Asia in the nineteenth century. This process continues today: 'there is a direct connection between the World Bank's drive to privatize communal lands and put an end to and devalue subsistence farming and the return of witch hunting in several parts of the world, like Africa, India, and more recently, Papua New Guinea'.[11] As such, accumulation by dispossession (to use David Harvey's theorisation of primitive accumulation as an ongoing process)[12] is not gender neutral but, rather, turns on the denigration and exploitation of women.

Extending Federici's analysis, we can see that increases in organised and interpersonal sexual violence follow the movement of capital. A 2019 report published by Canada's National Inquiry into Missing and Murdered Indigenous Women and Girls made clear the deep links between resource extraction and sexual violence. Mining projects and oil pipelines revolve around 'man camps' which house thousands of transitory workers, mostly from non-Indigenous communities.[13] There is ample evidence that these 'man camps' becomes sites for violence against Indigenous women and girls, for systematic rape, sexual exploitation, abduction, and murder, as well as for an increased demand for sex workers, often drawn from Indigenous communities. Delee Nikal, a member of the Witset Nation, a community belonging to the Wet'suwet'en band of five nations in northern British Columbia, states, 'they're transient workers who have no connection to us, but they have the backing of the police'.[14]

A similar dynamic can be seen surrounding military bases, with equally violent consequences. To give an example, in 2012, Agnes Wanjiru, a twenty-one-year-old Kenyan woman, is alleged to have been killed by a British Army soldier training at a camp in Nanyuki, central Kenya. Wanjiru's neighbour, Maryanne Wanjui, observes, 'We did not get justice because even after reporting, there was no action taken by police'.[15] In both contexts, women draw attention to the ways in which sexual violence is undergirded by the nation-state – by the police and the army, as well as the geopolitical agreements that broker resource extraction and the military-industrial complex. As Nancy Fraser argues, 'capitalist production is not self-sustaining, but free rides on social reproduction, nature and political power'.[16] In the widespread sexual violation that attends militarisation and resource extraction, we can see the work of the nation-state in securing capitalist social relations.

It is not only through processes of accumulation by dispossession, but also in the everyday management of labour that the state carries out or condones sexual violation. As we'll see in the example of 'virginity testing' at the end of this chapter, 'the production of a particular type of worker requires a particular type of family'.[17] The family, then, is a racialised category, used to facilitate and naturalise the differential exploitation of labour. Practices of statecraft – often violent, sometimes bureaucratic – enable and maintain the conditions necessary for extraction and exploitation. Sexual violence can function as part of the process of determining one's racial position. We can see this in the recruitment of native sex workers to service soldiers engaged in military occupation or in the widespread rape of enslaved women on plantations in the Americas. In returning sexual violence to its central role in the development of capitalism, we can see that though sexual modernity's story of the good life is crucial to the creation of racial groups, it does not operate alone, nor simply on the level of ideology. Instead, sexual modernity and the making of race depends not only on sexual respectability and the nuclear family, but on rape, sexual exploitation, and femicide.

## Foucault's Blind Spots

*What Foucault would have learned had he studied the witch-hunt, rather than focusing on the pastoral confession . . . is that such history cannot be written from the viewpoint of a universal, abstract, asexual subject.*

Sylvia Federici, *Caliban and the Witch*

The underbelly of sexual modernity does make some appearances in Foucault's analysis – in his analysis of clandestine sex between men and boys, for example. But for the most part, Foucault is concerned with the promise of sexual modernity, its ironic freedoms and generative restraints. Further, despite the tremendous range of his writing, Foucault's work is curiously gender-neutral, largely assuming what was true for men was also true for women. Though he wrote extensively on the nuclear family as the site for social control, the way in which the family served to organise social reproduction is largely absent from his analysis. To understand the ways in which gender functions within sexual modernity, we must consider the role of the family in securing capitalist social relations. As Friedrich Engels famously observed, the formation of the conjugal family, with a patriarch at its helm, at the advent of capitalism marked the 'world historical defeat of the female sex'.[18] This defeat was achieved by the destruction of the previous organisation of resources, in which, though labour was divided by gender and by age, women's work (and that of children) was an integral and plainly acknowledged part of the collective social world. Capitalism divided production from reproduction, turning the latter into the private, unpaid work of women. As Federici's work reminds us, this process was far from smooth or painless; it was the product of sustained violence and coercion.

This division of labour is not a minor aspect of gendered social relations that can be easily dislodged through men taking on domestic tasks; its privatisation and separation from the sphere of production is crucial to the processes of accumulation, expropriation and exploitation through which profit is made. As Fraser puts it, 'Wage labour could not exist in the absence of housework, child-raising, schooling, affective care and a host of other activities which help to produce new generations of workers and replenish existing ones, as well as to maintain social bonds and shared understandings'.[19] While, of course, the majority of women have worked – and continue to work – outside of the home across all phases of capitalism, the naturalisation of cleaning, care, cooking, and child-bearing as the natural domain of mothers helps to secure worse waged working conditions for women, as well as their continued exploitation through the 'second shift' of domestic labour at home. This naturalisation of social reproduction as women's work is crucial to the sexual dyad and institutions of heteronormativity around which sexual modernity takes shape.

Foucault's analysis of sexuality is also hopelessly Eurocentric, as scholars such as Ann L. Stoler insist,[20] tracing a genealogy through France and England but leaving their extensive empires out of the picture. To address this absence is not to 'add' the colonies for the sake of some kind of geographical 'inclusion', but to reveal the hidden racial dimensions of sexuality – the way that race and sexuality come into the world together, connected like a Möbius strip. As in the case of gender, the connections are not merely rhetorical but material. Race as a modern phenomenon emerges from colonial domination, which imposed racial categories on subject populations in order to extract land and labour. Natural sciences – botany, anatomy, zoology – were enlisted to confirm domination as natural and inevitable, based on a hierarchy of human, animal, and plant in which the European bourgeois man would be at the top. Crucially, racial difference was also ascribed to populations within Europe, with lower classes understood as a race apart from the emergent bourgeois elite. Sexuality was the means through which these differences were given salience, both through rhetoric and representation, which portrayed certain 'races' as biologically distinct and sexually deviant, and through attempting to determine who should have sex with whom and under what circumstances. In bypassing the context of colonial expansion within which the emergence of sexuality in Europe takes place, Foucault rehearses a crucial aspect of the Enlightenment philosophy that his oeuvre largely seeks to critique: the existence of the self as an autonomous, self-governing actor.

While Foucault attempts to reveal the processes through which the self is made, he obscures precisely the historical circumstances in which these processes took place. In my analysis, I move between colony and metropole, not only to return our understanding of sexuality to the global context of its emergence, but also – more urgently – to show the ways in which the sexual and the racial division of labour function together. Further, by returning the processes of accumulation, expropriation, and exploitation to our conception of modernity, we can begin to understand why the promise of sexual modernity is so powerful. In other words, if we understand the disavowed or hidden forms of violence on which capitalism depends, we can approach its sedimented story of self-realisation with a useful degree of scepticism.

Heeding Chitty's timely reminder that a set of bourgeois sexual norms did not become hegemonic purely through their adoption within the ruling class,[21] I suggest that active practices of statecraft were crucial to the use of these norms as metrics of racial difference. Further, while bourgeois sexual arrangements might be ideologically powerful, they have never been as widely adopted as their cultural overrepresentation might suggest. As Raymond Williams argues, 'no mode of production and therefore no dominant social order and therefore no dominant culture ever in reality includes or exhausts all human practice, human energy, and human intention'.[22] Though none, in Britain at least, live entirely outside its orbit, many eschew the promise of sexual modernity and find their sense of self, eroticism, and kinship elsewhere. My aim here is not to suggest that a set of sexual arrangements are adhered to by the majority, but to insist that the profound ideological dominance of these arrangements impacts us all.

The notion that a set of European bourgeois sexual standards was imposed on colonised people has gained some traction in recent years – indeed, this is an argument I take up to some degree in these pages. But this argument often relies on claiming precolonial sex/gender systems as 'radical' or 'progressive'. For example, when India finally repealed the anti-sodomy laws imposed on it under British colonial rule, some argued that this marked an anticolonial victory, one that might allow India to restore the 'fluid' sexual and gender norms that predated European empires.[23] I suggest a rather more circumspect approach to understanding the ways in which colonial rule transformed sexuality, sometimes by strengthening rather than dismantling indigenous patriarchies. There's little political use in claiming the superiority of precolonial sex/gender systems, not least given that in the Indian context, a virulent Hindu nationalism has come to power promising to restore India to its apparent former (precolonial) greatness. Further, it is clear from even a brief examination of South Asia's religious traditions that forms of patriarchy absolutely preceded colonial rule and that the gender identities outside of the sexual dyad (such as hijras) were subject to violence and exploitation as well as reverence. A critique of sexual modernity need not require us to falsely elevate precolonial or premodern sexual norms. Instead, we must try to understand how the colonial state exploited or reshaped pre-existing sex/gender systems to facilitate regimes of extraction.

A set of sexual norms was not founded in Europe and then violently exported to the peripheries; rather, as Rao observes, 'the very notion of the self to which sexuality attaches is itself an artefact of the colonial encounter'.[24] As such, we must be attentive to the ways in which centre and periphery were co-constituted – that the resources for the making of the self were themselves found in colonial expansion. The industrialised capitalist social relations within which the nuclear family became the basic unit of organisation were developed through the extraction of raw material from the colonies. The notion of manly restraint was articulated in dialogue with racialised masculinities that were viewed as dangerously uncontrolled; and the very idea of the free self who could elect to enter marriage took shape against the widespread sexual violence of slavery and colonial rule. Thus, to understand the light side of sexual modernity – its dazzling promises, its offer of care and comfort – we must also take a long look at its underbelly, at the gendered and racialised exploitation on which it depends. This is not to say that the promise of sexual autonomy and romantic love is meaningless, but to insist that we need a more expansive conception of sexual liberation, one that is articulated to the vision of a world without race.

As the myriad ways in which states regulate sexuality are too numerous to explore in this account (I give little space to discussions of contraception, for example), I focus on the regulation of sexual life in colonial India, at Britain's borders, and through the functioning of the welfare state, marriage laws, education, and counterterrorism. These practices don't merely reflect or reinforce pre-existing racial difference, they actively produce and maintain the complex social fiction of race. Let's now turn to the example of 'virginity testing' at the UK border, where we can see how acts of sexual violation – often made in the name of respectability, hygiene, and national security – are tied to the making of racial regimes.

## Virginity Testing

*They didn't do it to the women coming from Europe or Australia or*
*America, did they? I suppose it was just to prove that they had power in*
*their hands.*

*The Guardian*, 13 May 2011

In January 1979, a thirty-five-year-old Indian woman, who came to
be known as Mrs K, arrived at Heathrow Airport with the intention
of marrying her fiancé, a British resident of Indian descent. The
immigration legislation stipulated that anyone entering the country
as the fiancé of a British resident did not require a visa, providing
the marriage would take place within three months of arrival.
Though Mrs K met these requirements, on arrival at Heathrow,
immigration officials pulled her aside for further questioning. Her
advanced years piqued their attention: they assumed that in India
she would be considered too old to be unmarried. Immigration
officials suspected she was posing as the fiancé of a British resident
in order to evade immigration controls: they insisted she undergo
an invasive physical examination to 'check' she was a virgin and
therefore a 'legitimate' bride. She was not coerced into accepting
sexual modernity's story of the good life; instead, her body was
measured against the fantasy of Asian sexual practices drawn from
colonial governance. After a male doctor certified that her hymen
was intact, her status as a fiancé was deemed credible, and she was
given three months conditional leave to enter the country for the
purposes of getting married and settling with her husband in
Britain.

When *The Guardian* broke the story, it emerged that 'virginity
tests' were being conducted in British High Commissions across
South Asia as well as at Heathrow Airport. This news caused consid-
erable scandal, both in Britain and internationally. James Callaghan's
Labour government sought to minimise the effects of the outrage,
not least on Britain's relationship to India, its former colony, by
denying that the practice was widespread and officially mandated.

Though records are incomplete and difficult to piece together, we know that tens if not hundreds of women were subjected to this practice over the course of around a decade. In the years in which these tests were conducted, the arrival of South Asian women to the British mainland was a particularly fraught issue. Many were coming to join their husbands or fiancés who had arrived in the previous decade to work, following the path of wealth, resources, and opportunity from periphery to centre.

However, when the British government sought to tighten the borders, they were concerned about the numbers of single, South Asian men already in the country, fearing that these men would strike up relationships with white women. Conservative MP Sir John Smyth warned, 'If we do not allow families to come into the country as units we shall have all sorts of trouble with women. The female element is absolutely essential, and the sooner the men here have their wives with them the better I shall be pleased'.[25] Throughout the book, we'll see the state's continued preoccupation with the 'problem' of unmarried men, with the need to source women to provide sexual, domestic, and emotional services for social reproduction without disturbing fragile racial boundaries. In this instance, the government left a window open for 'family reunification' in the hopes that South Asian women would arrive to perform the role of racial containment, a role they presumed was dependent on sexual purity.

The fundamental assumptions on which the practice of 'virginity testing' were built were, first, that South Asian women would be virgins prior to marriage and, second, that South Asian women sought to evade immigration control. These assumptions were rooted in Britain's colonial governance of the subcontinent, through which anthropological insights mixed with racial paranoia to produce a powerful vision of South Asians as both naive and dangerous. Echoing centuries of colonial administrators, the British High Commissioner in Dacca, F.S. Miles, wrote, 'Bengalis, though friendly and likeable, are probably the most prone to invention and fabrication'.[26] A general view of the natives as wily and devious, always seeking to get one over on the British, translated into immigration policies and practices that placed South Asians seeking entry to Britain under tremendous suspicion. It is within this general field of suspicion that an obsession with South Asian women's virginity begins to make sense.

This preoccupation with virginity was built into the colonial criminal justice system, in which virgins were viewed as more credible rape victims than women who were sexually active. In 1888, Surgeon-Major Isidore Lyon insisted that 'medical testimony, important in every country, is especially so in the East, where it is often the only trustworthy evidence on which hangs the liberty or life of a human being'.[27] As such, the body – specifically genitals and breasts – rather than women's words were treated as the route to the truth. The fact that the state of one's hymen can hardly be considered proof of sexual history was obscured by the operation of power and authority. In the colonial context and at the border, South Asian women were viewed as both meek and devious, with a sexually demure appearance concealing an innately lascivious nature. And as Said makes clear, imperial power is maintained not by a brute assertion of cultural or racial superiority, but by these contradictory imaginings of the Other as they become embedded in policy, representation, and institutional life.[28] In other words, consent is as crucial as coercion.

In the case of Mrs K, her explicit consent to the examination is worthy of some consideration. 'Virginity tests' in High Commissions on the subcontinent were carried out as part of a larger medical assessment, apparently to check for contagious diseases, and without the requirement of written consent. Mrs K, however, was asked to sign a consent form. Though the internal examination was a form of sexual violation, it was carried out with putative consent. But to consider her consent freely given is to ignore the context; if she did not agree to the examination, she could not join her fiancé in Britain. Her virginity, then, was as important as her passport in crossing the border. Like a passport, it was taken as a sign of worth, authenticity, and legitimacy. Just as one cannot easily opt out of showing one's documentation, so she could not easily refuse to submit to this examination.

British authorities were well aware of the tenuous nature of contract at the border. As Chief Medical Officer Sir Henry Yellowlees wrote to P.J. Woodfield, 'surely the sanction applied to any potential immigrant who refuses to submit to medical examination . . . is simply to refuse him admission to the country?'[29] Yet the appearance of consent was crucial. As Mongia observes in her writing on the emergence of immigration control in the nineteenth century following the abolition of slavery, contract was crucial to navigating 'the central antinomy that haunted and shaped the nineteenth century: the distinction between freedom and slavery'.[30] As such, the very meaning of 'freedom' was at stake in the management of the global movement of people. The imperative to maintain the appearance of fairness – to secure consent, under duress, before enacting a violation – followed Britain through its transition from empire to nation-state.

In this example, we can see that the practice of virginity testing, though bureaucratic as well as violent, belongs to the underbelly of sexual modernity: it is part of the apparatus of statecraft that organises racial groups according to their assumed sexual arrangements. Virginity testing does not only respond to a set of racial myths but also sews these myths into the fabric of everyday life. A mythic story of the South Asian woman as fundamentally defined by her sexuality and its control at the hands of patriarchal men – the 'stereotype of the submissive, meek and tradition-bound Asian women'[31] as Pratibha Parmar puts it – became an ironic reality through her treatment by the British state. South Asian women had to submit to these tests (thereby confirming themselves as pliant and demure), sometimes to sign a consent form, and to testify to their virginity, because to do otherwise would bar them from entry to Britain. In other words, state practices do not merely respond to cultural ideas about racial difference – they also bring difference into being.

While the border offers a particularly stark example, we can trace these dynamics in other areas of public, social, and political life (education, housing, media, and so on). Across all of these arenas, we can see that practice and mythology work together; that fantasies of cultural difference act as an alibi for cruel acts of violation; that racial Others are measured against a set of bourgeois sexual norms; and that the 'race' is not a fact of nature but a human reality that requires tremendous work to make, remake, and maintain. Across all these areas, ideas about sexuality, gender, and family form the powerful dynamics and unstable heart of modern racial regimes.

# 2

## Sexual Science

### Lobsters and Penguins

*Dominance hierarchies are older than trees.*

Jordan Peterson

Jordan Peterson's 2018 self-help book *12 Rules for Life: An Antidote to Chaos* was an international bestseller.[1] Though he is trained as a clinical psychologist and teaches at the University of Toronto, he shot to fame through his YouTube lectures and Quora posts, both highly popular with young men. The basic methodological thrust of his approach is that we can find guidance for how to live a meaningful life in archetypes – in the figures and tropes of myth and theology. This idea is, of course, widely held; we read scripture, tell fairy tales to children, and watch Greek tragedy precisely because we imagine that in the archetypes found there, we will also find something of ourselves. Peterson takes up this logic; his 'rules' lay claim to an eternal wisdom. But a closer examination of Peterson's philosophy reveals a distinctly modern view of the world, one guided more by Social Darwinism and neoliberal maxims than by the ancients. Rule 1 – 'Stand up straight with your shoulders back' – begins with a lengthy discussion of the social and sexual lives of lobsters.

According to Peterson, the longevity of the lobster as a species makes it an ideal case study – being older than the dinosaurs, crustaceans can teach us fragile and confused humans a thing or two about survival. The secret to their endurance, claims Peterson, can be found in their adherence to strict hierarchies of dominance and submission. Lobster society stakes no claim to gender equality or sexual liberation; therein lies its success. Male lobsters fight for supremacy: 'The dominant male, with his upright and confident posture, not only gets the prime real estate and easiest access to the best hunting grounds. He also gets all the girls.'[2] Female lobsters, in turn, 'identify the top guy quickly, and become irresistibly attracted to him'. Peterson praises this 'brilliant strategy' and confirms it is precisely the strategy used by human females too, not to mention by the marketplace under capitalism, 'where the value of any particular enterprise is determined through the competition of all'.[3] For Peterson, the parable of the lobster opens up a great truth: dominance and hierarchy are natural and inevitable. They are facts of nature that must be respected, or we risk meaninglessness, decline, maybe even extinction.

While Peterson's logic might seem a particularly tendentious use of the natural world to defend a set of conservative gender roles, he is not alone in projecting social meanings onto animal life. Viewing the natural world as a legitimising mirror for human society is politically promiscuous, a method used to defend a huge variety of positions. Stories of 'gay penguins', for instance, regularly make headlines, with the saga of Roy and Silo at Central Park Zoo even inspiring a children's book called *And Tango Makes Three*, which is regularly subject to homophobic backlash when it appears in libraries or is taught in schools. The notion that the penguins are 'gay' makes visible the habit of viewing animal reproduction through the lens of sexual modernity – through romance, love, marriage, and family. And the backlash suggests that there's some significant power to be found in this anthropomorphising tendency. A similar set of projections can be seen in what Sam Solomon and Natalia Cecire refer to as the 'mycological turn'[4] – in the interpretation of fungi as the source of radical, even 'queer', potential. Across the board, we are compelled to defend our attachment to particular models of kinship as *natural*. To justify the organisation of society, we construct a narrative that makes the recent into the eternal, the possible into the necessary, and the contingent into the inevitable. We transfer the categories of 'man' and 'woman' across historical contexts and species;

we make the reproduction of lobster life a parable for proper gendered behaviour; and we 'validate' LGBT identities by using animals as a mirror for our desires.

Interpretations of the natural world have long acted as the foundational justification for human hierarchies. My concern is with the production of racial distinctions in particular, but I posit that hierarchies of race, gender, class, and sexuality emerge and become legible in relation to each other, and thus they must be explored in tandem and within a single – though complex and uneven – discursive frame. It might not be immediately obvious how this focus on natural sciences relates to the forms of racism which contour the lives of Asians in Britain, but this genealogy helps to uncover the structures of thought – the impulse towards taxonomy, analogy, and hierarchy – that continue to determine our collective consciousness. In order to understand how the categories of race, gender, class, and sexuality relate, we need to reconstruct their mutual constitution.

In this chapter, I'll start to reconstruct that history and trace the ways in which the focus on sexual reproduction (of plants and animals, as well as humans) in eighteenth century taxonomies laid the groundwork for the sexual politics of today's racial regimes. By tracing how the categories come into being together – in, against, and through each other – we can see how sexuality comes to be understood as at the heart of the self. This uniquely modern view of the self, in which sexuality is seen to express an interior essence, plays a crucial role in what Patrick Wolfe calls the 'mystical dimension' of racialisation.[5] With this, Wolfe draws our attention to the ways in which fragments of older cosmologies are woven into the fabric of sexual modernity, giving an emotional, aesthetic, or spiritual resonance to the brutal process of racialisation. This mystical dimension is also a mystification; it's the process by which race-making covers its tracks. In what follows, I attempt to uncover these tracks and follow them from the eighteenth century to the present day, to show how the structures of sexual modernity and the racial regimes they subtend have evolved.

## Taxonomy

*The centre of knowledge, in the seventeenth and eighteenth centuries, is the table.*

Michel Foucault, *The Order of Things*

The eighteenth century saw the emergence of the natural sciences, which were fundamentally concerned with classification, towards the ordering of all life into a table. To understand the gravity of this shift towards tabulated categories, we need to understand what predated it. Rather than a man-centred cosmology, the European Middle Ages were organised around the divine order, with both man and beast corresponding to the will of God. Pre-Enlightenment texts are full of stories of bodies doing things that seem impossible to us – wolves nurse human babies, men transform into women and back again, women take new shape as birds – because the culture/nature dichotomy had not yet been established; rather, there was 'a total system of correspondence (earth and sky, planets and faces, microcosm and macrocosm)'.[6]

In this system, the individual body is taken as a metonym of the wider cosmology. As such, the pursuit of knowledge – about plants, about animals, about physiognomy – was always, implicitly, the pursuit of the divine. Attempts to understand the natural world were attempts to 'uncover a language which God had previously distributed across the face of the earth'.[7] In this God-centred world, typology rather than taxonomy was dominant. Types are ideas, ideals rather than norms. As L. J. Davis points out, 'in a culture with an ideal form of the body, all members of the population are below the ideal . . . There is in such societies no demand that populations have bodies that conform to the ideal'.[8] Of course, this doesn't mean that all bodies are seen as equal. There is, in this time, what Thomas Laqueur refers to as 'a metaphysics of hierarchy' in which women are not the opposite of men, but their inferior; women are not a separate, complementary gender, but an unfinished, incomplete kind of man.[9] Gender relations, then, are premised on women's inferiority, but also on the notion that both women and men are imperfect or incomplete as compared to the divine. Other social distinctions – between serf and gentry, between child and adult, between clergy and congregation – were also justified as the God-given order.

It is with this epistemology that natural science marks a break. As David Scott puts it, the common story is that this is the time in which Europe 'leaves behind it the cramped intolerances of the damp and enclosed Middle Ages and enters, finally, into rational spaciousness and secular luminosity of the Modern'.[10] Natural science was a complex and contested part of this story in the eighteenth century, deeply imbricated in the colonial project, just as eugenics would be in the following century. Indeed, it was the process of colonial expansion that produced both the possibility and the need for a new man-centred epistemology. In the colonial encounter with difference, a logic needed to be established that would make moral sense of the subordination of subject populations and lands, during the period in which the notion of a universal human subject is beginning to take hold. This moral sense was no mere post hoc justification but the guiding principle of empire. The extraction and exploitation of resources – of land and of labour – depended on a view of the world that placed 'man' (specifically, the bourgeois European male) outside of and above nature. The responsibility of 'man' was no longer to act as custodian of God's earth, of which he was also a part, but to rule over it, to make the land productive, to maintain its natural hierarchies. Racial Others were part of the natural world, just like animals and plants, and to exploit them was both duty and destiny, as inevitable as tending crops. Taxonomy – a single science of order – gave this exploitation the weight of philosophy.

## Botany

*The blade (or stamen) does not unaptly resemble a small penis, with the sheath upon it, as its praeputium (prepuce). And the ... several thecae, are like so many little testicles.*

Nehemiah Grew

While the study of plants might seem an odd place to start, given their putative distinction from human society, botany occupied an important role in the development of natural science. As Foucault notes, 'Rousseau, at the heart of the eighteenth century, was a student of botany'.[11] From the Middle Ages through the Renaissance, in Europe plants were studied as medicines, but the eighteenth century saw the emergence of abstract and taxonomic study. Various systems emerged in this time to conceptualise and organise the influx of previously unknown plants, but Carl Linnaeus's system (published as *Systema Naturae* in 1735) was widely adopted after 1737 until the early nineteenth century. At the time of its emergence, taxonomic study was far from accepted by all natural scientists. French naturalist Georges-Louis Leclerc, Comte de Buffon, dismissed Linnaeus's system as abstract and contrived, 'merely a language, easy to learn and recite but contributing nothing to the knowledge of nature'.[12] Despite this opposition, however, Linnaeus's system gained prominence, and its influence can still be seen in texture of everyday life. The game 'animal, vegetable, or mineral?' is based on his *Imperium Naturae*, in which he established three kingdoms: *Regnum Animale, Regnum Vegetabile, and Regnum Lapideum.* Further, Linnaeus classified humans in his taxonomy, divided into regional groups – Europaeus, Asiaticus, Americanus, and Afer – and specified their respective 'phenotypic, cultural, and even characterological qualities'.[13]

The Linnaean system of classification is so important to the emergence of modern racial subjects not only because of his attempt to delineate these 'types' but because it marks a key inflection point in which sexual difference becomes central to classification. It had been observed before that plants reproduced sexually, but in the eighteenth century the new moral value of gender complementarity created the conditions for a reassessment of plant reproduction. Linnaeus ordered plants according to their reproductive organs: the first level of classification (the 'class') is determined by the number of stamens, the apparently 'male' part of the plant; the second level of classification (the 'order'), by the number of pistils, the 'female' part. Linnaeus described plant reproduction in sexual terms, taking the language and knowledge of human sexual reproduction as a model and metaphor, even though most plants have both 'male' and 'female' organs. As such, eighteenth-century botanists had to contort their logic to make the metaphor 'fit', reluctant as they were to conceive of plants as hermaphroditic. This notion could be instrumentalised for political ends. As Anne McClintock observes,

> the doctrine of sexual complementarity, which taught that men and women are not physical and moral equals but complementary opposites, functioned as an important supplement to nascent liberalism, making inequalities seem natural while satisfying the needs of European society for a continued sexual division of labour.[14]

That plant reproduction could be harnessed as an example of this complementarity in nature gave further weight to the call for gendered inequality as a moral good, based in natural law.

As Londa Schiebinger observes, 'the revolutions in science and sexuality cannot be understood in isolation, for they share an intimate history'.[15] The sexual parts of plants became seen as their 'essence' in line with the emerging view of human sexuality as an organising principle of the self. I propose that it is this resonance that allowed for Linnaeus's system to gain dominance over its competitors. The Enlightenment ushered in a new attitude to sex, made possible by viewing it within the prism of 'the economy of nature'. In the eighteenth century, the rise of 'affective individualism' reimagined the marriage relationship as one of choice rather than economic or social necessity.[16] As such, if even plants could be seen as husbands and wives by choice, the same 'choice' could be rendered natural in society.

The personification of plants and animals through the metaphor of human sexuality in turn justified human kinship arrangements through their apparent analogues in nature. In the poems of Erasmus Darwin, for example, plants became not only counterparts to sexed human bodies but were transformed into husbands and wives. And it was not only poetic licence that gave credence to this logic; even Linnaeus's own scientific writings tended to, as Schiebinger puts it, 'see anything female as a wife'.[17] In his explanation of the sexual system, plant 'marriages' are defined as either 'public' or 'clandestine', precisely the two categories which divided marriage in Europe until 1753, when Lord Hardwicke's Marriage Act insisted upon public proclamations of marriage. In the late seventeenth and eighteenth centuries, marriage in the popular imagination was transformed from arranged unions to partnerships based on love and affection. While marriages in Europe had primarily been seen as economic arrange-ments, brokering relationships between families, distributing labour and resources, and organising some aspects of both emotional and sexual intimacy, the emergence of 'companionate' marriage shifted the focus from the social function of marriage to its role in contain-ing one's intimate desires. Of course, marriage did retain an economic use – primarily that of disciplining unwaged social reproduction – but this function became viewed as an essential part of women's nature, as the fulfilment of an inherent feminine desire. As such, the ascrip-tion of the categories of husband and wife to plants carried with it the presumption of agency and morality, as well as reflecting a sense of marriage as a natural rather than social institution.

Botany was not considered a niche interest but a crucial epistemo-logical concern, integrated into political life. In this section, I have mapped out the ways in which botany was used to legitimise the promise of sexual modernity, its offer of comfort, respectability, and intimacy built on marriage. But botany was also entangled in the underbelly of sexual modernity, in the practices of violence, extrac-tion, and sexual exploitation through which the modern world was constituted. Between 1550 and 1700, the number of plants known in Europe quadrupled due to imports from the colonies, as imperial expansion continued apace and scientists took up key roles in colonial knowledge production. In 1768, for example, young botanist Joseph Banks (who would go on to become a colonial advisor and the director of Kew Gardens) was invited to join James Cook's Pacific expedition. Expeditions such as these would set the stage for Charles Darwin to travel on the HMS *Beagle* in 1831. The regular presence of botanists on colonial voyages, and the 'revolving door' between scientific and political pursuits is highly suggestive of the unique role of the natural sciences in the eighteenth and nineteenth centuries.

When Banks was on board a voyage to Tahiti, the cataloguing of flora and fauna went hand in hand with the development of a distinct colonial sexual culture. As Tahitians had no way to produce iron ore but a great need for it, the crew quickly began to exchange iron for sex, raiding the ship's toolbox and even pulling nails from the body of the ship itself. According to the crew's diaries, when the HMS *Dolphin* set sail from Tahiti, so much of the iron holding it together had been removed and traded that the integrity of the ship was compromised.[18] It is in the context of events such as these, events that characterise sexual modernity's underbelly, that we must situate the development of taxonomy, in order to see that scientific knowledge is not clean and objective but mired in a history of violence.

## Racial Categorisation

*The question of the humanity and rights of apes was intimately tied to the question of rights for women.*

Schiebinger

This development of botanical knowledge cannot be examined in isolation; it was pushed by and implicated within zoology and the study of anatomy, as well as the social changes in gendered relationships, noted in brief above. In this period, we saw the emergence of a two-sex model for understanding human variation. For centuries, the one-sex model had prevailed in Europe in which woman was viewed as an imperfect version of man; gender was a hierarchy, not a dyad, and was based on women's distance from men's metaphysical perfection. Gender was the primary category, and fleshy bodies were dynamic, shifting entities, capable of feats we cannot imagine in purely biological terms. The body was seen as porous, responsive to the external world, which acted on its humours with varying results, allowing some fluidity between gender categories. In contrast, the two-sex model that emerges over the eighteenth century is one that is rooted in the body, in a biological understanding of sexual difference. As such, 'The reproductive organs went from being paradigmatic sites for displaying hierarchy, resonant throughout the cosmos, to being the foundation of incommensurable difference'.[19] Men and women, like the male and female parts of plants, become opposites, brought together by the innate force of heterosexuality.

As these fields (botany, zoology, anatomy) developed in tandem, particular analogies were prevalent within the scientific community and took hold of the popular imagination. One of the key questions of the age was the distinction between human and animal. Both women and animals were seen as existing beneath the (white) man in the 'great chain of being', an idea with a long history: 'The notion that woman – lacking male perfections of mind and body – resides nearer the beast than does man is an ancient one.'[20] As such, the precise point of distinction between 'woman' and 'beast' had to be determined. When naturalists turned their attention to women and to female apes, they considered only sexual traits in their comparisons. Secondary sexual characteristics became highly overdetermined signifiers of development – for example, the breast and the beard were used to inform racial taxonomies. As such, in Linnaeus's taxonomy, humans were considered 'mammalia'. As Banu Subramaniam, a feminist historian of science, points out, 'even though mammals are defined by many characteristics such as hair, a four-chambered heart, a single-boned lower jaw, three middle ear bones, a diaphragm, and mammary glands, and although they all maintain a high body temperature, it is the feeding of the young that came to define us'.[21] Just as with plants, animal and human life was categorised according to sexual traits.

Investigations into sexual and gender difference were essential to the racial schema elaborated by the scientists of human variation. The hinge that was used to join the 'female' to the 'lower races' was the notion that both shared 'childlike' physical characteristics, which accounted for their inherent intellectual inferiority. The analogy was 'proven' through specific physical features, most notoriously the skull. Theories of evolution and natural selection (which I discuss more in the next section) provided another teleology on which to place 'females' and 'the lower races', both of whom were considered to share the 'slightly protruding jaw' of an ape and thus belong to a less evolved strata of humanity.[22]

This logic continues to exercise some power even into the twentieth century. The discovery of hormones was also slotted into the analogous frame, when Sir Arthur Keith interpreted racial difference as a form of pathological hormonal disturbance. As Stepan elucidates, 'So fundamental was the analogy between race and gender that the major modes of interpretation of racial traits were invariably evoked to explain sexual traits'.[23] It is this practice that makes clear the potential in analogy to function as a structure of thought assumed to be empirically true rather than a rhetorical device with explicatory use. Scientists regularly found data that did not adhere to either the analogy or the idea of an inherent difference or inferiority, which they explained away or discarded to keep the paradigm intact. To give an example, when scientists found women's brains were 'heavier in proportion to their body weights than men, giving women an apparent comparative advantage over men, [scientists] searched for other measures'.[24] The claim of scientific empiricism and neutrality legitimated the analogy as a fact and therefore allowed for insights into racial difference to be applied wholesale to sexual difference, or for class to be viewed through the same essentialising logic as race. We could think of this paradigm as what Arvind-Pal Singh Mandair refers to as 'the constant return of the imperial as the empirical'.[25]

In the current moment, analogy has fallen out of favour and is viewed as an anachronistic approach to identity, with 'intersectionality' acting as its replacement. While the turn away from producing knowledge through analogy is essential, we must still account for the ways in which analogy has produced the knowledge we intend to contest. The architects of the identity categories we take for granted could only give them any meaning *through* analogy; they always were constituted through one another, never standing alone. As Stepan observes, via Sander Gilman, 'the metaphor of blackness could be borrowed to explicate the madman, and vice versa. In similar analogical fashion, the laboring poor were represented as the "savages" of Europe, and the criminal as a "Negro"'.[26] In exploring the emergence of modern taxonomies – attempts to organise the whole world, animal, vegetable, and mineral, into a table – we can see that the flat, diagrammatic mode of viewing the world through the lens of intersectionality calcifies identity categories and, implicitly, the logic through which they come into being.

The emergence of racial categories cannot be easily disentangled from the reconstitution of the one-sex model into sexual dimorphism and attendant norms of gender complementarity. Sexual dimorphism – where the sexes of the same species exhibit different characteristics – becomes key to the modern human and was used to determine the boundaries of race and the fixity of racial categories. Though it might appear that the gender binary begins as a set of European standards, in fact, it produces new typologies in metropole and periphery at the same time. As Lugones notes, 'Colonialism did not impose precolonial, European gender arrangements on the colonized. It imposed a new gender system that created very different arrangements for colonized males and females than for white bourgeois colonizers'.[27] Being a woman and being a man mean radically different things depending on one's position in the racial hierarchy and the kind of labour one is expected or forced to perform. As Hortense Spillers contends, enslaved black women were not deemed 'women' as such; they were 'sexed' but not 'gendered'.[28]

Similarly, many racialised men were deemed feminine or passive – from the relative absence of beards in indigenous men in the Americas, for example, Europeans claimed that they menstruated. When faced with a different set of masculine norms in North African men, Europeans claimed they were more inclined towards homosexuality – and more barbaric as a result. The imposition of biological

sex doesn't necessarily homogenise gender roles, creating a model of
men and women that is the same across all contexts. Instead, it affirms
that a set of bourgeois norms around kinship, sex, and gender roles –
the respectable arrangements of sexual modernity – are at the
pinnacle of civilisation. In the establishment of this bourgeois script,
deviations in the organisation of sex, gender, and kinship come to be
conscripted as the basis for racial difference.

## Fantasies of Control

*We greatly want a brief word to express the science of improving stock,
which is by no means confined to questions of judicious mating, but which,
especially in the case of man, takes cognisance of all influences that
tend in however remote a degree to give the more suitable races or
strains of blood a better chance of prevailing speedily over the less
suitable than they otherwise would have had.*

Francis Galton

The developments in botany, zoology, and anatomy described above
set the stage for a new epistemology to take hold by the end of the
nineteenth century, a new way of understanding plant, animal, and
human within a single frame. This new consciousness of a single
planet rested on several key images and tools: the colonial map, the
'great chain of being', and the Family of Man. The colonial map
was a fantasy of flatness – a vision of a finite, feminised, knowable
world, available for extraction, cultivation, and development. The
'great chain of being', persisting from antiquity into the Middle
Ages, asserted that all beings could be classified according to a
hierarchy that moved from God to angels to humans to animals to
plants to minerals. The development of evolutionary biology does
not contest this image so much as offer a rationale for its perpe-
tuation. It is here that we see something of what Wolfe refers to as
the mystical dimension of 'race'; evolutionary biology brings with
it some of the old stories, giving new life to the idea of the 'great
chain of being', now articulated through the language of rationality

but with the old sense of the divine still offering some animating magic.

The idea of the 'Family of Man' developed at the same time. This image offered a way to understand the many objectified, commodified, studied, and taxonomised victims of colonial plunder as the wayward children of a European *paterfamilias*. As the father of the family was not considered entirely internal to the family structure but as its proprietor, this metaphor was sufficiently flexible to maintain both a sense of filial duty *and* the notion of discrete racial categories. These images had a temporal dimension, too: the colonies were deemed to exist in a different time to Europe, lagging behind in a civilisational teleology that still informs political discourse, policy, and geopolitics today. These images and tools gave an intellectual rationale to a system of dominance by integrating elements of an older moral economy – that of Christian Europe which viewed man as the steward of God's earth – into emerging scientific rationality. In this process, the imperative to steward divine creation is transformed into an imperative to produce: to extract resources, organise labour, and make profit – not to safeguard God's creation but to improve upon it.

These ideas came to the fore through the ascendancy of eugenics. Though we have come to think of eugenics as a relatively narrow field, reaching its brutal apex in the Nazi death camps, Subramaniam and other historians of science remind us of how wide-reaching and politically promiscuous eugenicist thinking was in the nineteenth century and continues to be today. We might think of eugenics in this broad sense as the application of scientific ideas for the improvement of society. Of course, what could be considered an 'improvement' was determined by those in power, who attempted to use science to maintain their position. Charles Darwin's theory of natural selection is the key inflection point. While Linnaeus's approach to variation was classification, Darwin sought to go beyond taxonomy; he attempted to explain how and why variation could arise, develop, and be maintained.

In the nineteenth century, Darwin brought observations from animal breeding into dialogue with classical economics (drawing heavily on Adam Smith and Thomas Malthus) to develop a vision of the world that was both orderly and competitive, rational and ruthless. Malthusian ideas of population control were given new rationality by Darwin's tracing of the same logic in the natural world, and Smith's 'invisible hand of the market' reappears in evolutionary biology through Darwin's idea of 'natural selection'.[29] Jordan Peterson continues this tradition in his apocryphal tale of lobster hierarchies, viewing the stock market as a continuation of the natural world's ruthless system of dominance. Darwin's cousin, Francis Galton, systematised many of these ideas in his theorisation of eugenics as the 'science of improving stock'. In its concern with reproduction as the mode through which biological traits are maintained, the focus on sexuality is entrenched, and eugenics targets women as the bearers of racial difference. For example, late nineteenth-century educators such as Kenneth Clarke campaigned against the education of upper class white women on the basis that their intellectual development would cost them – and the 'race' – their reproductive capabilities.[30] I'll discuss the role of eugenics further in chapter 4 to consider its role in welfarism and narratives of national decline.

The complex schema described above was re-articulated in a metaphor summed up by colonial adventure novelist H. Rider Haggard: 'In all essentials the savage and the child of civilization are identical.'[31] McClintock cites Ernst Haeckel, the German zoologist, 'whose catchphrase, "Ontogeny recapitulates phylogeny", captured the idea that the ancestral lineage of the human species could be read off the stages of a child's growth. Every child rehearses in organic miniature the ancestral progress of the race'.[32] The theory of recapitulation was used to justify racial hierarchy in which 'lower races' were viewed as the primitive past of the European man. As the adult, white male was taken as both ideal-type and norm, his former child self could be taken as a less developed, more savage version of that type. Anatomy created the 'evidence' to 'prove' this theory, securing a racial vision of human development and division, with vast and unpredictable consequences. White women, men and women of the 'lower races', as well as prostitutes and the white, British servant class, were viewed as primitive iterations of the proper human person, the white bourgeois man from the imperial centre.

## The Invention of Man

*Colonial science was not just about controlling the other – it was,*
*simultaneously, about defining the self and its place in nature.*

Kavita Philip, *Civilizing Natures*

As we have seen, over the course of the eighteenth and nineteenth
centuries, huge shifts took place, moving from a one-sex model to a
two-sex model, consolidating the idea of companionate marriage as
the ideal basis for kinship, and developing a sense of the individual,
albeit in the form of the white bourgeois man, as the fundamental
unit of society. From our contemporary vantage point, it is hard to
imagine a world without the individual, not least given the ways in
which access to this category has been widened, with women, racialised people, and children all seen as belonging to it. Yet, as many
have noted, the idea of the sovereign, autonomous self is not trans-
historical or inevitable. Wynter's work on the invention of 'Man' is
instructive here. She asserts that the sovereign, autonomous individual does not mark the limit of the human but a single model that
has represented itself as the human itself. We should note, however,
that this analysis does not necessitate a turn away from a universal-
ist humanism, but an insistence that this need not hinge on
self-realisation within the limits of individualism. Wynter traces the
invention of Man in two stages – the first (Man1) comes into being
through the early colonial encounter with the Americas, whose inhabitants were viewed as heathens, as outside of the paradigm of the
human. Man1 acts as the model for the secularised, scientific Man2
who is destined to dominate those who fall below him in the evolutionary chain of being.

We've looked closely at this second process, at the making of
Man2, and the crucial role of taxonomy in producing the figure
of the sovereign individual, the heroic subject of sexual modernity.
In tracing this history, we can see that the application of scientific
method to 'improve' society was widespread, and eugenicist principles
were embedded in social institutions. The idea of the 'survival of the

fittest' becomes crucial to the colonial project and has remained a key mode through which capitalist social relations are understood today, as Peterson's parable of the lobster indicates. Within and across these developments, the modern idea of 'race' becomes increasingly calcified. It is common to suggest that it is through taxonomy and natural science that 'race' as biologically determined comes into being, but I would like to suggest that something more complex emerges. Racial regimes are secured as facts through interlocking biological, metaphysical, and cultural rationales – all of which are given weight and meaning through the emerging discourse of sexuality. A modern view of sexuality as the motor that propels the self – a view that would be popularised by Sigmund Freud in the early twentieth century – began to take hold in this period, partially through these scientific developments. As Darwin's theory of natural selection inaugurates a new moral economy of biologically inherited characteristics, controlling the sexuality of subject populations became of increasing concern.

Here, I've mapped out elements of the dominant epistemology upon which sexual modernity rests. These ways of seeing, categorising, and making sense of the world were forged in the fires of colonial expansion. But the colonial project was not merely a set of theories, it was a set of practices – violent and extractive, but also bureaucratic and diverse, vast and particular. In the next chapter, I'll describe how the extractive project of colonialism controlled (or attempted to control) sexual behaviour using legal, military, and social means to produce and maintain scrupulous racial hierarchies.

# 3

# Racial Hygiene

## Sex in the Contact Zone

*They couldn't associate on deck with that touch of the tar-brush, but it was a very different business down here, or soon would be.*

E. M. Forster, 'The Other Boat'

E. M. Forster's short story 'The Other Boat' is set at the turn of the twentieth century, the apex of British colonial power around the world.[1] Lionel is trying to return to India to continue his successful career in the British Army and to reunite with Isobel, whom he intends to marry. On board the SS *Normannia*, he finds himself sharing a berth with Cocoanut, a 'Eurasian' youth, so named for his 'peculiar shaped head'[2] (though perhaps also for his unstable racial position), whom he met on the ship from India to England when they were both children. Lionel had spent his early childhood in India, until his father's sexual indiscretions provoked a split in the family, sending the children and mother back to the metropole. In the intervening decade between these two journeys, Lionel has become a decorated soldier. Cocoanut has had a rather more informal, though nonetheless effective, education in the nefarious workings of the shipping world, through which he is able to secure Lionel's passage and ensure, contra the usual scrupulous segregation of British officers from 'dagoes', that they are bunked together. As the ship travels east, the strict sexual and racial expectations of Lionel's mother, and the England she represents, recede. When the ship enters the Mediterranean, Cocoanut's attempts to seduce Lionel finally meet success and by the time they are sailing the Red Sea, 'they slept together as a matter of course'.[3]

At first, Lionel appears to be the embodiment of colonial masculinity: he is 'clean cut, athletic, good-looking without being conspicuous'.[4] Like his father (who, he informs his lover, was 'a hundred per cent Aryan'), his 'thick fairish hair, blue eyes, glowing cheeks and strong white teeth' are the very picture of the manly European. His physical appearance is matched by his temperament – 'His voice was quiet, his demeanour assured, his temper equable'[5] – and his success on the battlefield: 'he had got into one of the little desert wars that were becoming too rare, had displayed dash and decision, been wounded, and had been mentioned in despatches and got his captaincy early'.[6] He is quickly recognised as an insider by those aboard the ship who share his class position. This contingent of colonial elites 'make up two Bridge tables every night besides hanging together at other times, and get called the Big Eight which [he supposes] must be regarded as a compliment'.[7] He appears to embody the promise of sexual modernity, abounding in the qualities, of both appearance and character, essential to white bourgeois masculinity. Yet, he is shadowed by scandal. His father tarnished the family's good name by 'going native', taking off with his Burmese mistress and leaving his wife with five children to raise alone. Despite his horror at his father's dishonourable desires – and at the suggestion that he may have some unknown 'half-caste' siblings – his affair with Cocoanut is the source of deep pleasure, albeit crosshatched with shame and anxiety. Lionel's fear that he might have inherited his father's dubious proclivities precipitates the story's violent conclusion – to which we will return at the end of this chapter.

The two boats of the title – from India to England, England to India – are a metonym for the colonial project, a project that circumnavigated the world, creating and enforcing racial boundaries while also constantly producing the conditions for those boundaries to be crossed, fractured, or revealed as a fiction. In this chapter, I'll consider the ways in which colonial authorities attempted to manage forms of cross-racial contact and cross-class contact, particularly sexual contact. I use the term 'racial hygiene' as a means to understand these processes. While this term has largely been associated with Nazi eugenics, here

I use it in a broader sense to encompass the varied attempts to maintain the superiority of the 'ruling race', whether through state-regulated
sex work, prohibitions on marriage for private soldiers, or various other
means. Racial distinctions were fragile and needed to be consistently
shored up by policies and practices premised on the assumption that
sustained contact with the 'lower races' could contaminate British
stock. As some contact was necessary and inevitable, practices of racial
hygiene sought to choreograph and assign meaning to cross-racial
intimacy, to ensure hierarchies could be carefully maintained.[8]

Ships are what Mary Louise Pratt refers to as a 'contact zone', a
space of asymmetrical power relations in which different people and
cultures 'meet, clash and grapple with each other'.[9] As Marcus Rediker
and Peter Linebaugh's research into the revolutionary cultures of the
Atlantic reveals, maritime life was 'a multicultural, multiracial, multinational' affair.[10] Ships are both scrupulously hierarchical and
threateningly anarchic; they are spaces in which manifold sumptuary
codes attempt to prevent inevitable cross-class, cross-racial contact. As
such, these two boats are an apt theatre for this drama of inheritance,
in which institutions of racial hygiene (family, army, and patriarchy)
are threatened by figures such as Cocoanut, one of the wayward children of the British Empire, and the product of precisely the kind of
cross-racial union that preoccupied colonial administrations. While
white bourgeois masculinity may be at the top of the hierarchy, Forster
suggests this position might be more precarious than it seems – and
that for those at the top of any hierarchy, there's a long way to fall.

## Fit to Rule

*The sun was a mighty power in those far-off days and hostile to the*
*Ruling Race. Officers staggered at the touch of it, Tommies collapsed.*
                                    E. M. Forster, 'The Other Boat'

In the nineteenth century, as McClintock notes, 'the English middle-
class male was placed at the pinnacle of evolutionary hierarchy'.[11]
Indeed, his persistence as the paradigmatic figure of the human

continues into the contemporary era, albeit subject to increasing
scepticism. It is common these days to hear the 'straight white man'
marked out as a problem. Yet, despite this apparent scrutiny, many
fail to engage with the uncanny doubleness of this figure. As the
paradigm for the human, he is dependent on all kinds of non-human
or infrahuman others; as a norm, he is always on guard against
deviance from within or without. His power is precarious precisely
because it is dependent on the exclusion of those wayward or
discarded figures of modernity – figures such as Cocoanut in 'The
Other Boat'. Colonial governance went to great lengths to conserve
racial hygiene – to choreograph the ways in which people interacted
across the boundaries of gender, race, and class. As Lisa Lowe puts
it, 'The colonial management of sexuality, affect, marriage and family
among the colonised formed a central part of the microphysics of
colonial rule'.[12] I would add, however, that this kind of state intervention was not only addressed to the colonised, but to the colonial
elite. Said observes:

> When it became common practice during the nineteenth century
> for Britain to retire its administrators from India and elsewhere
> once they had reached the age of fifty-five, then a further refine-
> ment in Orientalism had been achieved; no Oriental was ever
> allowed to see a Westerner as he aged and degenerated, just as no
> Westerner needed ever to see himself, mirrored in the eyes of
> the subject race, as anything but a vigorous, rational, ever-alert
> young Raj.[13]

The fate of both ruler and ruled, then, is hopelessly intertwined.

Of course, the Hegelian account of subject formation is suggestive
of this dialectical constitution. According to Hegel, the autonomy at
the heart of the subject comes from its sublation of the Other, a kind
of internalisation through which the contradiction of Self and Other,
Master and Slave, is resolved through synthesis. In this process, all
that is dangerous and threatening about the Other is neutralised by
its role in the constitution of the Self. The Hegelian model, however,
doesn't account for the *perpetual* instability that shadows the

subject – the way in which this process is always incomplete. In other words, Hegel's is an ideal-type, not a historical account. As Lowe observes, the Hegelian dialectic 'established intimacy as a property of the individual man within his family':[14] through the subordination of women and children to his will, they become constitutive of his autonomy. Yet, as Lowe's work explores, in the colonies the patriarchal intimacy of the nuclear family, which turns on privacy, domesticity, and respectability, was intertwined with other, disavowed, spaces of intimacy. In colonial India, we might identify these disavowed intimacies as residing in the army barracks, the brothel, and the relationships between colonial elites and their concubines. These disavowed intimacies – those that constitute the underbelly of sexual modernity – threaten to undermine the stern boundaries of racial difference on which the imperial regime was staked.

The historical coordinates of the white, bourgeois, heterosexual man show the ways he is constituted through a particular vision of sexuality. This constitution, however, is highly unstable, as it both depends on and produces forms of sexuality it deems deviant or dangerous. According to Foucault, 'the bourgeoisie's "blood" was its sex'.[15] The aristocracy believed that its claims to superiority lay in the purity of its blood, a metaphor for inheritance. But from the mid-eighteenth century onwards, the bourgeoisie sought to assert its own fitness to rule. Its special character was assumed to reside in sexual restraint, marriage, and heterosexuality. These features measured its distinction from the unruly masses in both metropole and periphery, as well as from the decadent aristocracy. For Foucault, the emergence of this bourgeois self, whose fitness to rule was evidenced by the practice of a restrained heterosexuality, stemmed from a largely European process rooted in confession to a priest through which sexuality developed a clear narrative structure. As we saw in chapter 1, the kind of subjectivity produced by confession was developed and institutionalised through medicine, education, the nuclear family, and the wider organisation of life in Europe as it became increasingly industrialised.

As scholars of postcoloniality observe, however, the emergence of this self was intimately linked to racial science and colonial governance. Stoler, for example, observes the 'categorical effacement of colonialism' from Foucault's *History of Sexuality*, which turns empire into 'a backdrop of Victorian ideology, and contemporary stories about it, easily dismissed and not further discussed'.[16] Foucault's approach obscures the coproduction of the categories of race, gender, class, and sexuality. The search for what Foucault calls 'the truth about sex' was intimately tied to the search for 'the truth about race', as we saw in the previous chapter. The hallmarks of sexual modernity's initial promise (restraint, heterosexuality, choice, and marriage) must be read as forms of racial hygiene as well as sexual respectability. Sexual respectability is dependent, however, on sexual violence.

While British elites emphasised that it was their restraint, heterosexuality and marriage that differentiated them from the reckless lower classes in Europe and deviant racial Others in the colonies, the conduct of British soldiers, merchants, and bureaucrats tells a rather different story. Though there are many cases of individual sexual violence (such as the rape of native women by British soldiers) carried out with impunity, these acts were not the full extent of colonial sexual violence. Sexual violence and racial hierarchy were institutionalised together. The light side of sexual modernity – the ways in which it promised bourgeois men a life of respectability at the top of the racial hierarchy – depended upon a vast and complex underbelly which included a system of racially ordered and state-regulated sex work. In other words, respectability was an important fiction but rarely a reality: marriage took place alongside concubinage, romantic love never displaced its 'mercenary' counterpart, and while sexual restraint was lauded, rape was commonplace.

## The Management of Men

*Here was the worst thing in the world, the thing for which Tommies got*
*given the maximum, and here he was bottled up with it for a fortnight.*

E. M. Forster, 'The Other Boat'

British colonial control over India offers a particularly acute angle from which to observe the development of sexual modernity through the management of populations. While Portuguese, Dutch, French, and Danish-Norwegian powers competed for control over parts of the region, by the mid-eighteenth century, through what Mytheli Sreenivas describes as 'a combination of military victories, political negotiations with local rulers, and alliances with merchant groups',[17] the East India Company was established as the dominant force in the region. As the company expanded its mechanisms to extract resources, exploit labour, and subdue competitors to its authority (whether through building alliances, brokering deals, or dominating militarily), it began to function as a state. As such, it was the company that attempted to determine how soldiers, merchants, and missionaries would engage with natives according to gender, caste, class, and age. Attempts to choreograph these relationships were essential to responding to 'the native question' which, as Mamdani observes, described 'the problem of stabilising alien rule ... a dilemma that confronted every colonial power and a riddle that preoccupied the best of its minds'.[18]

In 1773, the company was brought under parliamentary surveillance, with further regulation enacted by Pitt's India Act in 1784. These interventions laid the groundwork for India to be brought under the direct rule of the British Crown in 1858, following the first cross-country armed rebellion against British rule the previous year, referred to by the British as the 'Mutiny'. In the shift from Company to Crown rule, new methods of statecraft – new ways to manage populations – were finessed, with a renewed emphasis on culture and consent. In this shift to Crown rule, the ethnographic state came into its own, as it was assumed that the uprising had been the result of slights to sensitive native cultural sensibilities. In particular, the story took hold that the uprising had been the result of bullets smeared with either cow or pig fat given to native soldiers to be used in the newly issued Enfield rifle, which required one to literally 'bite the bullet' before firing. As pigs are viewed as unclean by Muslims and cows as sacred by Hindus, it was assumed that this had offended native sensibilities. A more sober analysis points to the uprising as the inevitable political opposition to being ruled by an extractive foreign power. Though there were significant changes to the methods of statecraft employed in the different stages of colonial rule, they all met the problems of racial hygiene, sexual desire, and the messy and unpredictable ways in which people navigate the intervention of new power structures into their lives.

Colonial administrators – whether under the auspices of Company or Crown – sat in London (like their counterparts in Paris, Brussels, Amsterdam, and Lisbon) trying to determine who, many thousands of miles away, should have sex with whom and under what conditions. European men in India were there as company employees, soldiers, private mercenaries, missionaries, and independent traders looking to make their fortune. Though much of the everyday administration of colonial India was done by natives, the presence of European men was essential to the colonial project. They were needed to secure the extraction of resources – of tea, cotton, rice, minerals, and labour. While European domination was secured by force where necessary, for the relatively small numbers of European men to rule over the huge native population, the fiction of racial superiority was paramount. As such, the health, wellbeing, and appearance of European men was freighted with significance. In the colonial imaginary, women were needed to perform the work of managing the needs of these men, to reproduce the colonial workforce. Prior to the 1857 uprising, native women seemed to be the obvious choice. They were already there, after all. In a guide for East India Company soldiers published in 1810, Thomas Williamson explained that

> whether married or not, each soldier is generally provided with a
> companion, who takes care of his linen, aids in cleaning his

accoutrements, dresses his hair . . . These doxies do, certainly, now and then kick up a famous row in the barracks; but on the whole, may be considered highly serviceable; especially during illness, at which time their attendance is invaluable.[19]

In addition to providing sexual and emotional relief, native women could offer forms of reproductive labour tailored to the challenges of life in the colonies; that is to say, they could cook, keep a clean house, and launder clothes in a context that would have been unfamiliar, even threatening, to European women. In other words, they could do the work – sexual, domestic, emotional – of wives. Thus, British men in India were encouraged to take concubines.

Unsurprisingly, however, while solving the initial problem of the sexual, emotional, and reproductive lives of British men, this arrangement created a new problem: children. The children that issued from relationships with concubines had claims to British as well as native status. 'Eurasian' children – such as Cocoanut in Forster's short story – threatened the fiction of racial superiority, all the more when they issued from longstanding, quasi-marital relationships rather than from fleeting affairs or visits to sex workers. Emotional and social issues also sprung from these long-term unions – men became emotionally attached to their concubines, and some sought to include them in their inheritance, send their children to school or university in England, or to remain in India after the end of their contracts. The initial stabilising function of concubinage produced the seeds of its own unravelling. As such, in the transition to Crown rule, when racial divisions needed to be fortified, concubinage was phased out as official policy and bourgeois white women were increasingly relied upon to do the work of maintaining colonial elites.

After the uprising of 1857, short-service army contracts were brought in, with personnel drawn from among working-class populations in England – the 'Tommies' of this section's epigraph. These soldiers were an expensive resource in and of themselves, so their health and wellbeing were of financial and geopolitical importance. Marriage would have been the obvious solution to meeting the sexual and emotional 'needs' of these young men, as the ideal of gender complementarity discussed in the previous chapter gained moral traction. But marriage for soldiers, rather than only bourgeois colonials, was deemed too costly, both financially and in terms of the risk to racial hierarchy. European wives, even drawn from among the working classes, would need to be able to afford lifestyles that reflected the strict hierarchies of the colonial order. As Stoler notes regarding the Dutch East Indies, 'Company authorities argued that new employees with families in tow would be a financial burden, risking the emergence of a "European proletariat" and thus a major threat to white prestige'.[20]

Similarly, administrators viewed British soldiers as uniquely vulnerable – to the heat of the sun, to the deceptive wiles of the natives, to the sexual possibilities denied to them in Europe but endlessly available in the imperial peripheries. Working-class men were viewed as a distinct group – lacking in the qualities of manliness and restraint assumed to reside in bourgeois masculinity. As the acting district magistrate of Ahmadabad put it:

> Private soldiers are young men taken from the classes least habit-
> uated to exercise self-control – classes who in their natural state
> marry very early in life. You take such men, you do not allow them
> to marry, you feed them well – better in most cases than they have
> been accustomed to be fed, and you give them a sufficient amount
> of physical work to put them into good condition and no more. It
> is asking too much to expect that a large majority of such men
> will exhibit the continence of the cloister.[21]

It was feared that, in the absence of women, soldiers would turn to each other to meet their sexual needs. As homosexuality was also associated with racial degeneration – with the dangerous sexual excess and feminisation of the licentious East – it was vital to mitigate this threat. As Chitty observes, 'cultures of sex between men were politi-cized amid much wider forms of dispossession during periods of geopolitical instability and political-economic transition'.[22] Though Chitty's research does not consider colonial India, the concern with sex between British soldiers is illuminated by his framing. Concerns over sex between men viewed it as a key means by which venereal disease, already high among soldiers and assumed to originate with sex workers, could be further spread among the troops. This possibility threatened both the fiction of racial superiority and the viability of this 'costly import'. Concerns over homosexuality then, were also concerns over the economic efficiency of the empire. Hyam notes that 'Britain spread venereal diseases around the globe along with its race-courses and botanical gardens, steam engines and law-books'.[23] To stave off the threat of homosexuality and its attendant implications of degeneracy, women had to be found to meet men's sexual needs.

## The Registered Prostitute

*Sex had entirely receded – only to come charging back like a bull.*

E. M. Forster, 'The Other Boat'

The registered prostitute system in India was borne of the articulation of two propositions: the first, that men need sex; the second, that both the 'white race' and its claims to dominance must be protected. The sexual urges of young, unmarried, working-class men were thought to be uncontrollable in the licentious East. While interracial relationships threatened the fiction of racial superiority, prostitution – or 'mercenary love' – came to be regarded as a 'necessary evil'. Though the risk of creating a class of children with claims to British parentage were mitigated if they issued from paid sex, it entailed other risks that needed to be managed, such as venereal disease, which was a tremendous problem throughout the empire.

Scrupulous statistics regarding the rates of disease among the soldiers were kept, and discussions of venereal disease were a regular feature of parliamentary discussion in Britain.[24] Sex workers were deemed to be the origin of venereal disease, so it was them, not the men they serviced, that colonial authorities sought to control by means of regulation. While it may have been more expedient to inspect and treat the men themselves, as had been the case earlier in the nineteenth century, this practice was deemed bad for the morale and self-respect of the troops. It is notable here that though these men were drawn from the working class, in the colonial context they too could become bearers of racial superiority. While they were not required to *enact* the manners of bourgeois masculinity – class differences underpinned military hierarchy and were to be preserved, not dissolved, in the colonies – they were also not allowed to stray too far from their orbit.

Following the Cantonment Act of 1864, which organised sex work in military cantonments, the Contagious Diseases Act (CDA) of 1868 mandated, in major Indian cities and seaports, the registration of brothels and prostitutes, periodic medical examination of registered prostitutes, and detention ('treatment') in lock hospitals of those prostitutes found to be infected. A woman who resisted these measures was vulnerable to a fine or even imprisonment. Moreover, even though the CDA did not formally mandate residential segregation, in practice the registered prostitute system was an attempt to segregate brothels from the areas surrounding them and to ensure European-serving brothels were kept separate from native-serving ones. The law created two classes of sex workers – those reserved for Europeans and those who had sex with native men, of which only the former were subjected to forced inspection and registration. Political authorities even sought to mandate the attractiveness of the sex workers: in 1886, the quartermaster general of the British Army issued a memorandum calling for prettier sex workers for British soldiers serving in colonial India.[25]

Crucially, the registered prostitute system did not only impact sex workers, but all native women. Philippa Levine notes that in 1905, Lord Kitchener pronounced 'that all indigenous women likely to come into contact with British troops carry disease and that native women, as a group, are potential prostitutes'.[26] In collapsing the categories of 'Indian woman' and 'prostitute', the surveillance and violation of all Indian women became legally sanctioned to protect the health of the English soldier. Here we can see an earlier iteration of the logic that underpinned 'virginity testing' in Britain's immigration regime, with the British state's view of Indian women as deceptive and diseased institutionalising sexual abuse.

If we examine the Contagious Diseases Act in Britain as well as its imperial counterpart, some interesting dynamics come to the surface. While the CDA enacted in Britain limited registration to women whom the police suspected of prostitution (thus retaining the notion of sex work as something to be disrupted by the state), in India, prostitutes (albeit only those servicing Europeans) were required to register themselves. Colonial authorities considered the self-registration requirement harmless, contending that, in Hindu society, prostitution was a hereditary caste profession that did not attract shame the way it did in Britain. In a classic example of the tendentious colonial use of ethnographic knowledge, this assessment draws exclusively on the experience of upper-class courtesans, who occupied an auspicious, even if marginalised position, in India. This logic was used to preserve the 'government principle' of non-interference in religious and social custom in India.[27] By claiming that prostitution was, in all cases, a respectable, caste-based profession, the British authorities were able to manipulate native custom to serve their own ends, while also maintaining the appearance of non-interference. As Stoler observes, 'culture' was used 'to rationalize the hierarchies of privilege and profit, to consolidate the labor regimes of expanding capitalism [and] to provide the psychological scaffolding for the exploitative structures of colonial rule'.[28] As such, the sexual and the cultural intertwine to alloy a shield against the objections of both native and British reformers who saw British regulation of sex work on the subcontinent as a profound moral violation.

While the figure of the courtesan was used as an alibi for the registered prostitute system, actual courtesans fell victim to its invasive surveillance and violation. Tawaifs, women belonging to the highest class of courtesans, led a privileged existence during the Mughal era, which came to an end with British rule; in Lucknow, for example, not only were tawaifs listed in civic tax ledgers – a rare occurrence for women – but they were also included in the highest tax bracket. When the Mughal Empire ended, the status of tawaifs underwent significant changes. Since they had provided assistance to the 'rebels' in the 1857 uprising, they were punished by the British, who imposed heavy fines and penalties, including the confiscation of their property. It also became official policy to relocate the healthiest and most beautiful among them to cantonments for the enjoyment of European soldiers. As Talwar Oldenburg puts it, 'Women, who had once consorted with kings and courtiers, enjoyed a fabulously opulent living, manipulated men and means for their own social and political ends, been the custodians of culture and the setters of fashion trends, were left in an extremely dubious and vulnerable position under the British'.[29]

In this manner, we can see that the principle of 'non-interference' was, in fact, only a more elaborate and insidious kind of intervention through which colonial practices produced the realities they claimed were inherent to Indian culture. We should note, however, that the state's disruption of sex work in the metropole and its regulation of sex work in the colonies both served to marginalise sex workers, as well as to extend the carceral state's reach into the lives of all women. As we'll see in chapter 7, the premise that one can be saved is not always better than the assumption that one is beyond redemption.

It is worth pausing on the regulation of sex work, as it reveals a series of contradictions within colonial rule. In particular, the CDA and the management of venereal disease reveal the ways in which the fiction of race was fragile and bound up in ideas of health and hygiene, need and desire, cultural difference, and sexual hierarchy. Racial difference was not self-evident; racial regimes needed constant reproduction through the management of distinctions between Europeans and natives. As such, the growth of a 'Eurasian' population needed to be carefully contained to prevent further disturbances to racial hierarchy. The classed divisions among English men were also particularly threatening, precisely because the maintenance of white masculinity as an ideal was crucial to the justification of imperial dominance. Private soldiers, then, needed to be accorded some racial privileges without being given the financial means to maintain a conjugal family. According to Levine, 'The only means whereby soldiers could establish a place in the hierarchy of the colony was in relation to the natives, from whom they received a bewildering variety of specialized services, including sex'.[30] This instability – in which class position is tempered by racial hierarchy and racial hierarchy is maintained through the management of sex, including

state-mandated sexual violation – helps us to understand the continued imbrication of sex, class, and race.

In British rule over the Indian subcontinent, first by the East India
Company and then by the Crown, we can see the ways in which the
promise of sexual modernity and its violent underbelly work together
to maintain the fiction of racial superiority while always producing
a kind of threatening excess – whether in the form of illegitimate
desires, attachments, acts, or children – that could undermine the
legitimacy of colonial rule. In this process, we can see evidence of
Robinson's claim that 'the production of race is chaotic. It is an
alchemy of the intentional and the unintended, of known and
imagined fractures of cultural forms, and relations of power and the
power of social and cultural relations'.[31] Examining the various ways
in which men's sexual and emotional needs are understood and
catered to as a biopolitical imperative begins to reveal the diffuse
nature of state interventions. We can see that these interventions have
an improvisatory quality, with contradictory needs clashing as well
as sometimes finding a point of fragile balance. So far, from our
account, however, we have only considered the ways racialised women
were deployed to maintain the status of the white man. In the next
section, we'll consider the fraught and ambiguous position of white
women in British India.

## The Fallen Woman and the Memsahib

*Marriage or virginity or concubinage for Isabel?*
E. M. Forster, 'The Other Boat'

White women went to the colonies in fewer numbers and for more
varied reasons than their male counterparts. They went as missionaries, governesses, wives, and barmaids; they went in search of
marriage, of experience, and of adventure not available in Europe.
Like working-class soldiers, they were in a complex in-between position. White women were members of the racial elite but without many
of the opportunities for autonomy, domination, and pleasure afforded

to men of the same social standing. As Stoler observes, 'European women in these colonies experienced the cleavages of racial dominance and internal social distinctions very differently than men precisely because of their ambiguous positions, as both subordinates in colonial hierarchies and as active agents of imperial culture in their own right'.[32] As we see with the figure of the Eurasian, the in-between is crucial to our understanding of imperial governance; it is where the *work* of upholding racial regimes becomes visible. It is also in these in-between characters – those who shore up white bourgeois masculinity while also, always, threatening to undermine it – that we can catch colonial race-making in the act.

Across the board, whether they came as missionaries or sex workers, white women were viewed by colonial authorities as the bearers of the white race. There's also some evidence they saw themselves in this way. Mary Procida's work on colonial biographies suggests that in autobiographical narratives of the English in India, bourgeois writers regularly present their personal narratives as fundamentally intertwined with – and as justification for – the colonial project. She notes that memsahibs (the wives of the colonial bourgeoisie) tend to present themselves as 'die-hard imperialists' and suggests that this is because their 'lives in the Raj offered them a unique opportunity to construct existences of public interest and political significance',[33] an opportunity in short supply back in the metropole.

Despite this sense of political importance, for the English women who came to the colonies as wives (whether to officers, civil servants, or other men involved in the colonial project), life revolved around the domestic sphere and exclusively European social clubs. This confinement reflected their role – they were there to uphold the white race. Victorian whiteness 'was an extraordinarily ambitious social project', as Alastair Bonnett observes. He reminds us that 'it made enormous demands upon its progenitors'. The demands on white women were particularly acute. As such, the contact between memsahibs and natives had to be scrupulously limited and carefully choreographed in comparison to European men, who were afforded a little more freedom. As Vron Ware puts it, '[white women] not only symbolised the guardians of the race in their reproductive capacity, but they also provided – as long as they were of the right class and breeding – a guarantee that British morals and principles were adhered to in the settler community, as well as being transmitted to the next generation'.[34] For bourgeois white women in the colonies, respectability and domesticity, then, were just as crucial as performing sexual labour.

The central role of the memsahib is underscored in Forster's short story, in which Lionel's fear that his mother – the memsahib *par excellence* in her devotion to racial hygiene – might find out about his relationship with Cocoanut is the most potent iteration of his anxiety: 'behind Isabel, behind the Army, was another power, whom he could not consider calmly: his mother . . . There was no reasoning with her or about her, she understood nothing and controlled everything'.[35] The responsibility borne by the memsahib was counterposed by an omnipresent sense of threat to her body and dignity and, by extension, to the racial regime she was understood to represent. Graphic and debased stories of white women's violation by native men channelled the contradictions of colonial rule and the perpetual risks of 'the native problem' into a sexual script. As Ware observes, 'Whether as Mothers of the Empire or Britannia's daughters, women were able to symbolise the idea of moral strength that held the great imperial family together. In their name, men could defend that family in the same spirit as they would defend their own wives, daughters or sisters if they were under attack'.[36] This symbolic value was undergirded by everyday life among the colonial bourgeoisie, in which the myth of native men as sexual aggressors was used to control the mobility and social freedom of white women, determining where they could go, with whom, and for what purpose. As such, control ran in two directions: white women were subject to control *and* used to limit contact between white men and native women. The racial weight of gender complementarity, calcified by natural science, was essential to the management of the colonial elite.

In her writing on European women in colonial Nigeria, Helen Callaway observes that 'the question of European women's "sexual fear" appears to arise in special circumstances of unequal power structures at times of particular political pressure, when the dominant

group perceives itself as threatened and vulnerable'.[37] Her analysis
tracks with the British response to the 1857 uprising, in which violent
and debased stories of white women's violation at the hands of native
men circulated – in the metropole as well as among Europeans in
India – as evidence of Indian depravity. Ware recalls a story that
circulated in the *Englishwoman's Review and Home* newspaper: 'On
finding the remains of one of General Wheeler's daughters, the men
divided up every hair of her head between them and took a solemn
oath to kill as many "natives" as each strand of hair in revenge for
her unspeakable fate'. As Ware goes on to summarise, 'The colonized
people were to be made to punish and pay for their revolt against
colonial rule, but the severity of the punishment was given the
appearance of legality by being carried out in the name of avenging
the womenfolk'.[38] The apparent depravity of Indian men served to
justify the imposition of direct rule on the subcontinent, shifting
power from the East India Company to the Crown.

These stories continued to circulate in popular narratives in Britain
well into the twentieth century, with even the Runnymede Trust,
whose remit is 'racial equality', quoting a paper in 1974 claiming
'Pakistanis are disproportionately involved in sexual offences'.[39] Stories
of Asian men raping white women have tremendous purchase in
contemporary periods of political crisis too, as we'll see later in relation to the moral panic surrounding 'grooming gangs'. In the context
of 1857, however, we might also observe that the focus on white
women as victims of native male sexual aggression were partly to
deflect from the violence experienced by white men – their humiliation
at the hands of native rebels – as well as the violence they enacted.

The trope of respectable white women – mothers and wives and
governesses and missionaries – as potential victims of native sexual
depravity was shadowed by a figure more disturbing to the colonial
administration and who haunted British rule in India: the white
prostitute. As Levine explains, 'The European prostitute, by her very
presence, challenged white supremacy in distinctive and critical ways,
which reveal dramatically and vividly the importance of sexual
politics in colonial rule'.[40] Just as the native prostitute could figure
as a stand-in for the sexual availability of all racialised women, sex

workers of European extraction threatened the notion of white womanhood as uniquely vulnerable and in need of protection.

Colonial authorities dealt with the challenge of European sex workers in British India in two ways. First, they subjected European prostitutes to greater surveillance than their Indian counterparts, including, crucially, through segregation along racial lines. Increased control of white women in the colonies was enabled by emergent twentieth-century ideas of 'white slave' traffic that, despite evidence to the contrary, constructed white sex workers as helpless victims. Meanwhile, the internal trafficking and overall condition of Indian sex workers, who were economically worse off than Europeans, went largely unnoticed. At the same time, it has been argued that the presence of white sex workers played a key role in imperial feminists' fight against the CDA in India. Second, while exercising control over European prostitutes and brothels, British officials symbolically distanced themselves from them. They did so by reporting that most of the European prostitutes in India were either Roman Catholics or Jews from Central or Eastern Europe – and that even the few that were British were of Jewish heritage.[41] As such, European sex workers were racialised within the colonial project, given a distinct and denigrated racial position, through which the colonial elite could attempt to maintain the moral function of white womanhood as the elevated symbol of racial hygiene.

## Intimate Threats

*[Lionel] March has been a monster in human form, of whom the earth was well rid.*

E. M. Forster, 'The Other Boat'

Even in this relatively brief sketch of racial hygiene in colonial India, it is clear that the demands of sexual modernity acted upon a wide variety of political subjects, operating in distinct but connected ways on those deemed worthy of sexual freedom and those viewed as in need of excessive control. In this schema, the white bourgeois man is the paradigmatic figure of the human – the apex of modernity, of rationality, and of freedom. Freedom is particularly crucial, as it is in the tension between freedom and restraint that sexuality is harnessed as the foundation of being and, as such, as the privileged marker of racial difference. Sexual freedom – the freedom to choose one's partner and to resist forms of sexual deviance (such as sustained cross-racial intimacy, homosexuality and masturbation) therefore acts as a guarantee of freedom *tout court*. As such, we can trace the gradations of freedom – and therefore the complexities of racial hierarchy – in the kinds of freedom granted to the vast cast of characters (divided by race, gender, class, caste, and other markers of status) that found themselves in British India. Of course, even the kind of sexual freedom granted to those at the top of the hierarchy is highly limited, operating based on a constrained and utilitarian vision of intimacy and desire.

I suggest that the putative autonomy of the white bourgeois man – his modernity, his freedom, his status as a subject – is entirely dependent on his Others. This dependence is not only rhetorical, in that the self is always constituted by exclusion. Rather, white men in the colonies were literally dependent on natives and white women for their very survival, and this dependency was often negotiated through sexuality. White wives were required to maintain their husbands as respectable, bourgeois subjects. As George Webb Hardy put it, 'a man remains a man so long as he is under the gaze of a woman of his race'.[42] For white men of a lower status, native sex workers were sought as a lesser evil than homosexuality. For all, native men were a form of sexual threat and unmanly deviance against which colonial rule had to be secured. Sexual modernity comes with its own ironic undertow: its dependence on sexual violence and exploitation threatens to undermine the racial regime it is intended to secure. In this instability, we can see that racial regimes are complex social fictions rather than inherent realities; like all systems of power, they take tremendous work to make and maintain, and they are never totally secure, always producing new contradictions, new gaps and fissures, which cast doubt on their legitimacy.

At the end of 'The Other Boat', as the ship nears the port in Bombay, the full force of his own threatening desires – the gravity of the risk to his class, his future, his reputation – begins to overwhelm Lionel. The manifold tensions between being 'disturbed and disturbing', powerful and powerless, respectable and abject become unmanageable as the story hurtles to its tragic conclusion. First, he realises that he has left the door to their shared cabin unlocked – and that rather than share his sense of terror, Cocoanut is relaxed, knowing that there is little scandal that cannot be smoothed over with a bribe. He then goes up to the deck for some air and finds himself among his own 'caste', among Europeans whose presence is crucial to his sense of self: 'How decent and reliable they looked, the folks to whom he belonged!' It dawns on him that if his relationship with Cocoanut was to be revealed, 'he would become nothing and nobody'.[43] The racial regime from which he derives his sense of self is more precarious than it first appears – following the wrong desires is enough to undermine it.

Just as he renews his commitment to marry Isobel and thus have his position among his own fortified by the presence of a memsahib, he finds himself in conversation with Colonel Arbuthnot, who reveals that Cocoanut had secured his own passage through 'a fat bribe' in order to seduce him. When he returns to the cabin with this information, he tries to end things with Cocoanut. Unable to resist, they have sex, and at the climax, Lionel strangles his lover and throws himself into the sea. Though in this final act, Lionel reasserts his power over the 'subtle, supple boy who belonged to no race',[44] but doing so becomes the ultimate symbol of his lack of restraint. In his unbridled desire and subsequent suicide, he becomes 'a monster in human form' of whom his mother never speaks again.[45]

Examining the governance of British India has shown the ways in which the making of race depends on the management of sexual practices – on deciding not only who has sex with whom, but also attempting to determine where sex takes place, whether it is mediated by money, what significance it is assigned, and what status any children that issue from it will be granted. The management of sexuality was intertwined with the notion of 'culture' as a unique, distinct, and ahistorical force. Through the strategic use of the principle of 'non-interference' in native custom, sexual practices were transformed into the key metric of cultural difference. The European bourgeois norms of marriage, family, and sexual restraint were celebrated as the ultimate sign of civilisation – that which distinguished Europeans from natives, respectable from rough. Yet, these norms – the light side of sexual modernity – were only one half of the story. The treatment of native women – their subjection to invasive gynaecological assessment, their detention in lock hospitals – was as crucial to the maintenance of racial hygiene as the myth of the sexually pure and vulnerable memsahib.

Following these dynamics from the colonies to the metropole, we can track the shifts in sexual modernity from the empire to the nation-state. We'll explore the ways in which colonial interventions into native kinship calcified 'culture' and 'tradition' and turned marriage into a metric of civilisation. We'll then turn to the indistinct end of the British empire and its attempts to maintain imperial power in a postcolonial world. The arrival of 'immigrants' from South Asia transported old colonial anxieties about miscegenation, racial superiority, and imperial idealism to the border. In particular, we'll consider how the family is used to mediate this transition and fortify the racial regime of postcolonial Britain. Exclusion from the institution of the family – with its connotations of obligation, loyalty, and care – becomes a highly effective tool for both the immigration regime and the welfare state.

# 4

# National Family

## Women and Welfare

*The problem of infant mortality is not one of sanitation alone, or housing, or indeed of poverty as such, but is mainly a question of motherhood.*

George Newman, *Infant Mortality*

In 1965, A.J.P. Taylor ended his *English History 1914–1945* with the claim that in World War Two, 'the British people came of age. This was a people's war . . . Imperial greatness was on the way out; the welfare state was on the way in'.[1] This narrative – in which the hardship of war becomes the foundation for a centralised, universal, and democratic welfare state – is integral to the myth of a collective, unified British national life. As David Edgerton notes, 'The idea that the post-war Labour government created the welfare state out of little, and that it did so in the wake of the great popular mobilization of the war, dies hard'.[2] This myth turns on the premise that healthcare, education, social care, unemployment benefits, and so on are possible precisely because they are limited to citizens. In connecting this myth to World War Two, fantasised as Britain's moment of national greatness, the more complex realities of imperial decline and global migration can be displaced by a simple story of national unity.

The postwar welfare state, however, built on earlier forms of welfarism. Even the birth of the National Health Service, the most iconic and beloved facet of British welfarism, was initially a reorganisation of existing services rather than their dramatic extension. If we return to the turn of the twentieth century, a key moment in the development of modern welfare policies in Britain, we can see that many aspects of social services were neither borne from democratic concern for the wellbeing of the poor nor from working class agitation, but were interventions organised around the principle of national strength. Just as in colonial India, the British state sought to manage the domestic and sexual lives of the population on the mainland. As in the colonies, sexual habits, domestic arrangements, and kinship structures were sites of anxiety and intervention: they needed to be controlled to conserve racial hygiene and ensure imperial dominance.

In the late nineteenth and early twentieth centuries, the British government was highly concerned with the 'health' of the population, with worries about both numbers and 'quality' of 'British stock' occupying significant political space. In the aftermath of the second Boer War (1899–1902), Britain's disastrous military performance was the source of anguish, with concerns that racial degeneration was to blame. This concern over the 'quality' of British soldiers was particularly acute given that the Boer forces were far fewer in number but much more effective on the battlefield. According to historian Anna Davin, in this period, 'population was power'.[3] Britain had to compete with other imperial powers, not least Germany, whose populations were healthier, as well as to maintain racial superiority over subject populations. The unusually consistent presence of foreign correspondents covering the Boer War ensured that the protracted and bloody conflict was prominent in the metropole. During the seven-month siege of Mafeking, for example, correspondents sent frequent updates to newspapers detailing the daily life of the inhabitants. This level of awareness helped to cement widespread fears that British men were lacking in the manly virtues and physical prowess needed to defend the empire.

In response to this concern, the government set up an Inter-Departmental Committee on Physical Deterioration, which operated on the assumption that the health of the ordinary citizen formed the basis of military power. Just a few years earlier, Sir Frederick Maurice articulated this concern, insisting that the army 'ultimately depends' on the 'national staple'.[4] As such, on the assumption that strong and healthy working-class men would be needed to defend Britain against

both rival colonial powers and subject populations, welfarist interventions sought to manage the health of the ordinary citizen. As we
see in Foucault's theorisation of biopolitics, the individual connects
to the population at the level of sex because sex is the initial vehicle
for the reproduction of life. To exercise control over the national
population, one must intervene in the sexual lives of individuals. He
describes biopower as power concerned with 'life itself'. On the level
of the population, this is a power concerned with 'propagation, births
and mortality, the level of health, life expectancy and longevity, with
all the conditions that can cause these to vary'.[5] If the strength of the
soldier is ultimately found in the health of the citizenry, biopolitics
intervenes as a form of military optimisation.

Women were targeted as the bearers of national strength. Working-class women were increasingly viewed as bearers of British
stock – as essential to the national polity, rather than as peripheral
and dangerous. They were being drawn into the folds of an emerging
'whiteness'. The eugenicist ideas we encountered in chapter 2 formed
the bedrock of the interventions that followed. Despite the widespread
acknowledgement that the brute facts of poverty (poor housing,
pollution, overwork, and so on) contribute to high infant mortality
rates and ill health, mothers were the target of eugenicist attempts to
'improve' the race. Most of the state interventions took the form of
surveillance and advice rather than money and housing. Health
visitors were appointed to conduct home visits and advise on matters
of cleanliness, clothing, and feeding; 'hygienic milk depots' were set
up to provide sterile milk for bottle-fed babies; and schools taught
temperance and cookery classes. As such, a veritable army of 'experts'
(via voluntary societies, hospitals, local councils, or schools) sought
to transform the structures of working class life to more closely
resemble the family in its bourgeois form, organised around conjugal
marriage, male breadwinners, and mothers as childrearers. Though
these early reforms implicitly capture the importance of social reproduction, they do so to support national strength rather than family
life or women's health for its own sake.

Eugenicists viewed marriage as foundational to racial hygiene and
sexual respectability. The shifting emphasis on gender complementarity

as a matter of racial distinction is particularly important: a manual
from the 1860s aimed at young women insists that the purpose of
marriage is for a man to protect and guide them, while an equivalent
publication from 1914 claims that marriage is needed to reproduce
the race, maintain social purity, and offer mutual comfort to both
partners.[6] This idea of conjugal marriage as the basis for national
strength tied sexual respectability, bourgeois kinship structures, and
racial hierarchy into welfare interventions. As Davin observes, 'the
terms in which reforms were proposed also involved reference to
the nation, the empire, or the race, and in this way might be rendered
acceptable which otherwise would have smacked of socialism'.[7] This
narration, however, is not a post hoc justification for socialist policies,
but evidence that welfare policies are double edged, used as tools of
domination that can nonetheless distribute access to the means of life.

While the welfare state is often understood as stemming from a
democratic impulse towards redistribution, practices of state welfare
are highly varied, informed by multiple, sometimes competing, rationales. The same services – pensions, healthcare, education – can be
funded and delivered in radically different ways and understood
according to different narratives. Nadine El-Enany and others remind
us, for example, that the wealth from which British public services
were built came from the extraction and exploitation of imperial
domination. The explicit relationship between welfarist reforms, marriage, and racial hygiene also serves another function in the making
of state power. In knitting together social services and national
strength, the welfare state consolidates the distinction between citizen
and non-citizen. Often framed as a dwindling resource that must be
preserved for the citizen and kept from the migrant, we can see that
welfare provision is highly ambiguous, neither inherently oppressive
nor liberatory. As we'll see, marriage and family are key mechanisms
through which access to welfare provision is filtered.

The conjugal family is assumed to exert a stabilising influence: it
organises desire and intimacy, as well as social reproduction. Of
course, our desires, our intimacies, always overspill this container.
But nonetheless, the moral weight of the family as a metric of civilisation is powerful precisely because the family can be a source of

comfort and meaning. Family is used as a filtering device, used to determine entry to Britain and access to particular social benefits. This access is racialised: welfare provision sorts us into categories, divides citizen from non-citizen, single person from family unit, child from adult. As such, all sorts of unruly elements – immigrants, working-class people – find their kinship practices scrutinised to determine their entitlements. If we return to Goldberg's description of the racial state, we can observe that through welfare and border policies, the state shapes 'spaces and places, groups and events, life worlds and possibilities, accesses and restrictions, inclusions and exclusions, conceptions and modes of representation'.[8] Through these biopolitical processes, the nation becomes imagined as a family composed of families, and non-citizens are mythologised as a threat to our most intimate connections.

## Metaphors and Metonyms

*They found themselves strangers in their own country, they found their wives unable to obtain hospital beds in childbirth, their children unable to obtain school places.*

                    Enoch Powell, 'Rivers of Blood' speech

The idea of the 'family' does tremendous political work; it can determine one's position in the racial hierarchy, organise social reproduction, and act as a container for intimacy, desire, money, and power. The colonial order had been premised on Britain assuming a patriarchal role in the 'Family of Man'. As in the Victorian ruling class household, in which the patriarch existed at a slight remove from the family, acting as its proprietor rather than one of its members, the British state was meant to hold its subject populations at arm's length, still connected by law but out of sight. The rule of law was promoted as a universal, essentially egalitarian mode of governance – a fair, paternal justice – in which all the empire's subjects could expect the same even-handed treatment. As Partha Chatterjee observes, however, the assertion of universalism went hand in hand with instating the colony as an exceptional space where liberal principles could be suspended in what he refers to as the 'rule of colonial difference'.[9] At the height of the anticolonial movements, the need to maintain these liberal illusions was even more acute, as Britain sought to hold on to its global power as a world of putatively independent nation-states came into view.

The metaphor of the family that had been so effectively deployed to characterise the empire – with Britain in a parental role and its colonies as dependent children – could be redeployed as a national story rather than an imperial one. Of course, Britain's 'domestic life' remained as tied up in a set of global connections after formal decolonisation as it was at the height of its empire. These ties were not a matter of accident but design. Britain sought to maintain its global power through the Commonwealth, another space in which the familial metaphor was deployed with clear racial aims. In 1949, the newly elected Australian prime minister, Robert Menzies, asserted that Australians are not only 'citizen[s] of Australia' but of the Commonwealth, which he described as 'our ancient family association, unique in history, the love of which is bone of our bone, flesh of our flesh'.[10] This sense that the white dominions retained a familial connection to Britain despite being many thousands of miles away, while British subjects arriving in the 'Mother Country' from Caribbean or African parts of Britain's empire were strangers, makes visible the shifting racial function of the family metaphor.

The notion of the national family has a long history. We can take Basilikon Doron, the 1599 treatise on government by King James VI of Scotland (later he also become James I of England) as an early modern example, in which he insists, 'Just as no misconduct on the part of a father can free his children from obedience to the fifth commandment (to honour one's father and mother), so no misgovernment on the part of a King can release his subjects from their allegiance'.[11] In 1941, George Orwell addresses this theme, albeit for a different purpose, describing England as 'a rather stuffy Victorian family . . . a family with all the wrong members in control'.[12] The bonds of loyalty and obligation through which we understand the family can be deployed to demand allegiance to the parental figure of the ruler, as per the Basilikon Doron, but in its more modern incarnation, the notion of the national family is used to strengthen two other kinds of loyalty: first, to the abstract idea of the nation, and second, to one's fellow citizens. In Orwell's use of the metaphor, he hopes to show how this loyalty could be redirected in service to socialism. The political promiscuity of this metaphor is crucial, as it is this ambiguous and dynamic quality that allows for its racialising function to seem like common sense.

The use of the family metaphor to make sense of nationalism's racial exclusions was particularly effective when it became attached to postwar welfare policies. As Bonnett argues in 'How the British Working Class Became White', 'Welfare came wrapped in a union jack'.[13] In the postwar period, the explicit logic of racial hygiene from the aftermath of the Boer War was displaced by a story of national unity. Gail Lewis confirms the ways in which the state's responsibilities were organised through the racialising metaphor of the national family:

> We were responsible for those that we did not know – the 'strangers' – as long as they were within the nation, within the boundary, this naturalised form called the nation. And of course that would be ranked in terms of male breadwinners and dependent wives and children. You'd get child benefit (called family allowance then) paid to the woman because she gave birth. It was a framework of benefits organised around the construction of a naturalised gender order.[14]

The family, then, has a metonymic relationship to the welfare state: the nation is assumed to be a family of families, with the bonds of responsibility, obligation, care, and discipline this image implies.

As I've noted elsewhere, the vision of happy and respectable, implicitly white, nuclear families can be found in Beveridge's vision of the welfare state, 'with the family allowance and national insurance designed to supplement and bolster the fragile nuclear household'.[15] While feminist organisers, such as the Wages for Housework campaign, demand that women's unpaid work should be remunerated, we should be clear that the Family Allowance (later called the

Child Benefit) was delivered to support nuclear households rather than to pay women for their work. Though feminist organisers defended the Family Allowance and campaigned for its extension, particularly in the face of attempted cuts in the 1970s, there was deep division within the movement as to what the money was for – whether women were obliged to spend it on their children or whether it was theirs to use as they liked.[16] These debates within the feminist movement draw our attention once again to the political instability of welfare, the way in which state services are always contingent and contested. They are a key site through which the fulfilment of our needs (for money, education, healthcare, housing and so on) becomes tethered to the nation-state system with its attendant racial hierarchies.

Postwar welfare policies continued to organise populations through the management of gender roles and family units, rewarding respectability and penalising those who were unwilling or unable to meet the demands of sexual modernity. As such, as well as offering services and support, welfarism also disciplined the wayward or deviant back into socially acceptable and economically productive family units. The state's sovereign power to remove children from families looms large in the experience of welfarism, as the implicit threat that subtends even the seemingly benign or supportive services through which people encounter the state's power. Whether one's performance of sexual modernity's scripts – of respectability, conjugal marriage, and gratitude – is convincing is a matter of serious consequence.

This metonymic connection between the family and the welfare state animates nationalism's exclusions by casting racialised outsiders as a drain on national services. Of course, in accessing state services, few feel that they are in the receipt of *familial* care. In fact, the disciplinary dimensions of the welfare state are often entirely apparent in the experience of going to the job centre, the GP surgery, and the housing office, in which the legitimacy of one's familial and sexual life is in constant question. Further, accessing particular aspects of state welfare – 'claiming benefits' – is often a highly stigmatising experience, as I'll explore more in the next chapter. Nonetheless, the idea that the welfare state belongs to the national family has taken on a mythic quality in Britain's racial regime. The epigraphic quotation from Enoch Powell's 1968 'Rivers of Blood' speech offers an important touchstone. While the apocalyptic imagery of Powell's speech has received the most attention, it is in its more prosaic images – of a man unable to secure a hospital bed for his pregnant wife or a school place for his child – that its lasting power is found. Here we see, in stark and enduring terms, a demonstration of Sivamohan Valluvan's argument that 'nationalism is able to press any number of sleights of hand, whereby ordinary xenophobic racisms obtain an enmeshing and defensive innocence'.[17]

## Movement and Marriage

*We have strong reasons for not treating husbands and wives in exactly the same way in the granting of unrestricted right of entry. In the Bill, as in our nationality law, we have assumed that the husband is the head of the family and that the wife acquires his domicile.*

Mr David Renton, Minister

As the imperial order of European empires gave way to the new geopolitical norm of nation-states, questions of migration and mobility shifted. Just as the family was used as a metric of civilisation to determine one's position within the national hierarchy, so too was it deployed at the border to determine entry to Britain. But this form of constricted mobility was not an immediate effect of the emerging nation-state system. Rather, Britain as a bounded national entity had to be constructed from its imperial form. Through the tense, protracted, and indistinct end of empire, a new national racial order emerged in which former imperial subjects found themselves outside of the contract of citizenship.

In order to maintain its position of global dominance in the era of decolonisation, Britain passed the 1948 British Nationality Act, which granted an imperial form of citizenship to millions of people around the world, allowing millions of black and brown people from across the declining empire to live in Britain.[18] This marked a continuation of the norm of mobility characteristic of the nineteenth century, which was dominated by empire-states, rather than the far more restrictive movement of people in the twentieth-century nation-state system. By granting rights of entry and residence to its former colonial subjects, Britain attempted to maintain the myth of imperial unity and equality in the age of anticolonial struggle and successful movements for national independence. While it is often understood that Commonwealth migration was sought to fill the postwar labour shortage, in fact, most labour recruitment schemes were aimed at Europe and the settler colonies, so as to maintain Britain as 'white'.[19]

This period of relatively open postwar immigration was short-lived, however, as the arrivals from the Commonwealth were greeted not as kith or kin but as 'the insinuating ghosts of a colonial world supposedly separate from domestic British life'.[20] The British state soon moved to introduce controls targeted at colonial subjects from the Caribbean, Africa, and South Asia. Both the liberal illusions of empire and the rule of colonial difference, however, reasserted themselves in immigration law, which sought to exclude Commonwealth citizens without appearing to instate a colour bar. Successive pieces of legislation in the 1960s began to chip away at freedom of movement within the Commonwealth, culminating in the 1971 Immigration Act, which introduced the idea of patriality – only 'patrials', or those born in Britain or with a parent born in Britain, had the right to enter and stay in Britain with no restrictions on their movement or employment. While the legislation made no explicit reference to race, in 1971 a patrial was most likely (98 per cent) to be white.[21] As Luke de Noronha argues, 'racist immigration and nationality laws had to be made racelessly, without reference to race'.[22]

Tightening up immigration controls presented a problem, however, for the British state's desire to prevent interracial relationships. Most migrants from South Asia in the previous decades were single men. If they remained in the UK, there was the risk that they would not remain single for long. As we saw in the discussion of virginity testing, South Asian women coming to join their husbands or fiancés were seen as key to a strategy of containment. Their sexual labour was required to preserve racial boundaries, containing the desires of

South Asian men and acting as a barrier – at least in Britain's racially ordered imaginary – between South Asian men and white women. Therefore, as Rachel A. Hall notes, South Asian women arrived as dependents on men: they were here to perform sexual and domestic labour – to do reproductive work within the home and to prevent South Asian men from seeking white women for this work.[23] As their immigration status was dependent on their sexual labour, it was as gendered and sexual subjects that their legitimacy was assessed. In the conscription of South Asian women for a strategy of containment, we can hear an echo of the role of the memsahib in colonial India, there to ensure racial hygiene.

A window was opened for marriage migration and family reunification with the aim of producing 'a "manageable" minority comprised of homogenous nuclear family units of migrants who were economically productive yet socio-politically reserved'.[24] The conjugal or nuclear family was viewed as a viable object of state management, whereas the extended or corporate family represented a threat to social and political stability. As Helena Wray observes, extended families are viewed as dangerously antidemocratic, associated in the public imaginary with honour killings, forced marriage, and excessive control over women and children. Immigration law reflects this preference for the conjugal family form, with financial support from the extended family being discounted in spousal visa application, even though in the wider British population, financial support within families is an ordinary occurrence.[25] As such, migrants find their own kinship practices under surveillance and reshaped under the guise of maintaining the supposed norms of the nation, even though these norms are themselves highly contested.

Marriage migration, however, quickly came under heavy scrutiny. In 1969, there was a total ban on men coming as husbands from the Commonwealth. As Parita Trivedi notes, 'The ban on male fiancés was presented as a benign act by the government to "protect" young Asian women from the "horrors" of the arranged marriage system'.[26] Yet, simultaneously, the government suggested that British Asian women marrying men from the subcontinent ought to emigrate to join their husbands. As the 1978 parliamentary Select Committee report insists, 'we believe that the members of those minorities should themselves pay greater regard to the mores of their country of adoption and indeed, also to their traditional pattern of the bride joining the husband's family'.[27] Notably, this custom, though common, is hardly universal in South Asia. Though the ban on women sponsoring their husbands or fiancés was soon overturned by the courts as discriminatory, it is indicative of the charged classificatory nature of the border, in which migrants are sorted into categories of gender and kin (as husbands and wives rather than merely men and women) and assessed accordingly.

In 1977 the Primary Purpose rule was introduced. A controversial piece of legislation, it was presented as a means to address the apparently widespread (but never evidenced) 'abuse' of the visa system by South Asians. It required migrant husbands to prove that the primary purpose of the marriage was not to gain admittance to the UK. There were various tweaks to the Primary Purpose rule from 1980 onwards, after significant legal challenges and public consternation. Exemptions were made for women citizens born in the UK or with one parent born in the UK to sponsor husbands, as the law was impacting the 'wrong' constituencies, including white British women. In 1983, the law was amended to allow naturalised women citizens to sponsor a spouse, but it also shifted the burden of proof onto the applicant, who had to prove their marriage was not to evade immigration control. In 1985, following a legal challenge to the gendered discrepancies of the law, the court found only that the rule was discriminatory to women. Instead of abolishing the rule, however, the government extended its application to male sponsors.

These laws were putatively race-neutral. They appeared to apply the same gendered expectations to all, regardless of country of origin. In practice, bureaucratic discretion relied upon racial myths developed by the colonial administration and re-energised by the demands of national governance. Immigration officers were perfectly aware that migration was a fraught political issue – that there was the fear of a 'flood' of foreigners – and that they were to play their part in stemming this imagined tide. As such, marriages that did not conform to the expectations immigration officers held of South Asian customs were subject to increased scrutiny and higher rejection rates. It was assumed that women who appeared too timid were being manipulated into sponsoring a visa. Women who appeared too confident were also heavily scrutinised, as South Asian women were understood to lack agency. Given this maddening bind, sometimes even when applicants fulfilled all the necessary criteria, they would nonetheless lie on applications in order to conform to the cultural expectations of immigration officials.[28] In the insistence – sometimes in law, sometimes in its application – that South Asians conform to the modes of kinship and gendered embodiment expected of them by the British state, we can see the continued power of ethnographic conceits in the production of racial difference.

It is clear from even a brief examination of immigration law in the postwar period that not only are assumptions about South Asian sexual life built into processes of bordering, but that these processes produce certain kinds of subjects. People are sorted into categories of kinship and gender as well as nationality and age, and they must make themselves legible to the state through these categories, becoming properly raced as well as gendered and sexual subjects in the process. Crucially, however, these processes do not proceed in a simple, orderly fashion from a unified and homogenous state machinery. If we track what Radhika Mongia refers to as the 'the microscopic, almost surreptitious, global transformations of the empire-state into the nation-state',[29] we can see that there is an improvisatory quality to the way in which the state intervenes into the personal lives of those seeking to cross its borders. The imperative to maintain race-neutral language and the appearance of liberal universality contradicts the imperative to limit migration. Expectations regarding kinship, gender, sexuality, and intimacy are mobilised in an attempt to resolve this contradiction, but each attempt at resolution produces a threatening excess which itself must be managed. In this chaotic, haphazard fashion, racial regimes are made and maintained. Attempts to determine the kinds of relationships into which people enter are never wholly successful; though the state can reward and punish, it cannot determine the ways in which people will attempt to inhabit or resist the categories into which they are sorted.

## Who Can Have a Family?

*The family is the natural and fundamental group unit of society and is
entitled to protection by society and the State.*

                    Article 16(3) of the Universal Declaration of Human Rights

There are few institutions as powerful as marriage and family. They
are naturalised through sexual modernity, and we come to imagine
them as ahistorical and inevitable. This naturalisation obscures the
ways in which companionate marriage and the conjugal family take
on a new, modern shape, organising our labour, our affection, and
our sense of self in line with the imperatives of managing populations
and resources. This critical approach, however, should not obscure
the fact that family life does genuinely offer care, comfort, joy, and
meaning for some. Welfare provisions and the family wage allowed
many, though never all, workers 'to form relationships, create homes,
care for loved ones, recuperate before recommencing work, and
perhaps even raise children'.[30] These opportunities do not represent
sexual liberation, but they ought not to be dismissed too easily; leisure,
love, and rest, even if only for a few, are no small victories. In harnessing itself to the metaphor of the family, the nation-state becomes
the protector of – and proxy for – our most intimate relationships,
our most powerful sense of home and safety.

   So far in this chapter, I've tried to show the vital role of family in
the making of race by examining key state interventions into marriage
practices. The interventions into the lives of working-class women in
Britain after the second Boer War were part of a system of governance
in which the conjugal family and devoted mother were yoked to the
health of the nation. In the second half of the twentieth century,
family and marriage continued to determine access to resources – to
citizenship, work, the welfare state, and national belonging. This
freighting of the conjugal family with racial significance has continued as the nation becomes viewed as a family of families. As Lewis
notes, 'racialization is a compound process that gathers into itself and
is inseparable from discourses of gender and sexuality'.[31] Marriage

and the family are part of this compound process, bringing disparate elements – economic, emotional, physical – together within a single institution.

Marriage forms a crucial part of the Hegelian dialectic, which sees modern freedom as the process of self-realisation through possession – first of one's own interiority, then of the external world through labour, and then through contract. As Lowe argues, 'Property, marriage, and family were essential conditions for the possibility of moral action and the means through which the individual will was brought consciously into identity with the universal will, expressing the realization of true "freedom" rather than mere duty or servitude'.[32] The notion that the family acts as a guarantor of freedom is, of course, a gendered one: it is men, not women or children, who 'possess' the family and can access self-realisation through this possession. The freedoms promised by sexual modernity thus depend both on those included within the family and those deemed pathologically beyond familial intimacy.

To be part of the national family, one must be capable of having a family oneself. While South Asians are considered to do marriage and family incorrectly – too patriarchal, too uncontained, too mercenary – others are excluded from these institutions altogether. The production of blackness as the ultimate Other of white respectability rests upon precisely this exclusion, with black family structures viewed as highly pathological and lower black marriage rates as evidence of a unique antipathy to the institution. These tropes originate in plantation slavery, where marriage between black men and women was largely prohibited, making explicit the relationship between marriage and freedom.

This notion of blackness as beyond or against the family continues to shape the contemporary racial regime. The most well-known twentieth-century proponent of this notion of black familial pathology is Daniel Moynihan, an American sociologist whose 1965 book, *The Negro Family: The Case For National Action* (commonly known as the Moynihan Report) has influenced generations of policy makers on both sides of the Atlantic. Moynihan posits that black poverty in the United States is the result of matriarchal family structures that emasculate men and undermine proper conjugal family units: 'at the centre of the tangle of pathology is the weakness of the family structure'.[33] This idea recurs in contemporary Britain, with 'black criminality' attributed to absent fathers and dysfunctional families. As Adam Elliott-Cooper observes, Black conservatives consistently put forward these arguments, offering a 'post-racial alibi to reheated imperial racisms'.[34] Though surveillance, policing, and incarceration serve to disrupt family life, the pathologisation of Black kinship presents these mechanisms as akin to *parental* discipline: the state's authority is needed to compensate for the absence of paternal authority in the home.

The view of black life as chaotic and degenerate, running contrary to the conjugal family and its promise of freedom, is used not only to criminalise black communities, but also to deport black Britons. De Noronha's insightful work on deportations to Jamaica reveals the way in which the majority of young men who have grown up in Britain as non-citizens and who face deportation are compelled to fight their removal on the basis of Article 8 of the European Convention on Human Rights: the 'Right to respect for private and family life'. De Noronha explores the difficulty these young men facing deportation have in making their relationships legible as familial, caring, and meaningful to the courts or the Home Office. As he elucidates, 'in deportation appeals, some relationships are more legible than others, and legal determinations invariably mobilise race, gender and class–based stereotypes surrounding intimate and family relationships'.[35] Many of the men about whom he writes do not have stable, paid employment but perform the labour of social reproduction: they cook, clean, and take care of children, even when they don't officially cohabit with their partners or children. Yet the essential work of care is viewed as insignificant when undertaken by the 'wrong' person – the gendered script of respectability demands that men take on formal, paid work.

Though sexual modernity has redefined respectability around a more 'equal' division of labour, with women across the class divide joining the formal workforce, marriage and cohabitation remain the legible script that signals responsibility and attachments. Even as fewer and fewer people are able or willing perform this script, even as austerity undermines the few protections left to the nuclear family household, the old story of gender complementarity and sexual respectability continues to be used as a tool of race-making.

Racialisation does not take place in a binary fashion; rather, the racial order is multilayered and racialised groups take shape in relation to each other, not just in relation to 'whiteness'. The notion that the black family is a contradiction in terms takes shape against the notion that Asian family structures, with their immutable traditions and patriarchal power structures, are a threatening alternative source of authority. Both a deficit and a surfeit of family becomes a troubling form of deviance, requiring state intervention of a more violent and invasive fashion than that of welfarism. The division of the world's people into racial categories is a form of ordering that depends on these multiple axes of difference, on hierarchies that shift and change according to an evolving and unstable set of criteria.

In part I, I have traced the development of sexual modernity to explore the ways in which it is comprised of both violence and opportunity, connection and alienation, new ways of being and new forms of discipline and control. The promise of sexual modernity and its disavowed violence come into the world together: the promise of self-realisation for some rests on the exploitation and constructed infrahumanity of others. As we have seen, it takes tremendous work – scientific, bureaucratic, military, cultural – to make race. Shifting now to the end of the twentieth century, in part II of the book, we'll see how race-making shapes life in contemporary Britain. While the techniques of colonial statecraft (such as indirect rule) often reappear, new forms of biopolitics come to the fore, particularly through neoliberalism, the War on Terror, and austerity. With these developments, new forms of uncertainty are rife: the nuclear household, the sexual dyad, and the couple form are all losing their capacity to organise our lives. As they fray, the cruellest techniques of race-making (deportation, citizenship-stripping, incarceration) intensify. While there are some liberatory possibilities in the fraying of these arrangements, these are not evenly distributed. For example, while the hold of the

sexual dyad is loosening its grip, access to support for gender transition has been decimated by austerity. Further, reactionary political
movements tied to globally networked nationalisms are seizing the
political opportunities represented by these uncertainties.

In the next chapter, I'll turn to New Labour, which made highly
effective use of gender, sexuality, and the family. I'll consider the
party's extension of gay rights as an iconic form of inclusion in the
national polity, which served to justify an expanding regime of
exclusion, punishment, and immiseration for those viewed as incorrigibly resistant to sexual modernity. As we'll see, gay marriage is a
profound political development precisely because sexual modernity
depends on marriage as a symbol of freedom rather than restraint.

II

# 5

# Divide and Assimilate

## Cutting Edge with Money to Burn

*Tony Blair has done more for LGBT rights than any UK politician.*
*Whatever your politics, he's a gay icon.*

Tom Burke, national co-chair of LGBT Labour

*Queer as Folk* aired in the UK on Channel 4 in February 1999. Written by Russell T. Davies, it was hailed by *The Guardian* as the 'first gay drama on British TV'. The eight-episode series unfolded with a relentless comic energy. Revolving around Manchester's gay village, *Queer as Folk* follows the lives of three men – Stuart, Vince, and Nathan – as they navigate sex, work, family, love, and friendship. Rather than being an incidental backdrop, a vibrant, confident, commercial gay culture is at the heart of the programme. The characters who inhabit this culture function as archetypes: Stuart is the playboy – rich, handsome, arrogant; Vince, a *Dr Who* obsessive who works as a manager in a supermarket, is his long-suffering sidekick, admirer, and best friend; Nathan is a Stuart-in-the-making, a cocksure teenager quickly learning that being young and handsome is real currency on 'the scene'. A supporting character, Lance, is a straight African man (his country of origin is not specified), who is marrying Romey, a lesbian, to obtain a visa. Stuart tries to stop the marriage because he feels it will endanger his paternity rights, as he is the father of Romey's baby. At end of the first series, Lance is arrested and threatened with deportation after Nathan reports him to the Home Office in an attempt to win Stuart's affections. When confronted by the police, Lance lashes out, punching two officers in the face. The show's most likeable character, Hazel, Vince's mother, comments to Romey, 'do you want a man like that living with your kid?', thus cementing Lance's inferior position in the programme's moral economy.

This watershed programme in British television functions as a prescient parable for New Labour's political philosophy. Led by Tony Blair, New Labour sought to make a 'historic break' with the political orientation of the traditionally left-wing party in favour of what Seumas Milne described as 'an unconditional embrace of the new rules of the globalised economic game'.[1] *Queer As Folk* aired less than two years into Blair's government and shared something of the energy of New Labour. Though New Labour had many critics, accounts of the period almost universally refer to a sense of optimism in 1997, with the entropy and scandal of John Major's government giving way to a project organised around being 'modern' and 'progressive'. Though this upbeat rhetoric came with Labour implementing highly reactionary policies, in 1997, the end of a long period of Tory rule brought some hope that Britain could shake off its atmosphere of terminal decline.

With its relentless, driving, extra-diegetic theme music, fast-paced editing, and focus on individual potential (whether sexual, social, or economic), *Queer as Folk* captured the 'structure of feeling' of the late 1990s. The gay lifeworld depicted in the programme is not the left-wing, militant political culture of Lesbians and Gays Support the Miners or ACT UP – indeed, the show was criticised for largely ignoring the AIDS epidemic – but a culture organised around commercial bars and clubs. While homophobia persists in the show, it is framed as prejudice to which individuals respond. In *Queer as Folk*, they do so through outlandish and highly entertaining acts of revenge. For example, when a car salesman tries to steer Stuart in the direction of buying a more 'masculine' car (suggesting the sport is for gay men who are 'cutting edge with money to burn' but who shouldn't be taken too seriously), Stuart drives a Jeep through the glass showroom window. Individual acts of resistance – ideally performed with style – are viewed as the only viable way to respond to stigma.

Lance's presence on the programme coincided with the figure of the 'bogus asylum seeker' gaining wide purchase as a distinctly New Labourite scapegoat. In the late 1990s and early 2000s, Britain's moral panic about migration was channelled into this folk devil, inherited from the last days of Major's rule but used to far greater effect by Blair. Headlines denouncing people seeking asylum as fakes, criminals, rapists, or murderers, offered a powerful story of a national polity under siege, while the moral panic surrounding benefit fraud suggested a dangerous enemy within. As Bridget Anderson observes, 'those who claim benefits are increasingly subject to public excoriation that parallels the excoriation of migrants'.[2, 3] As we saw in the last chapter, welfare is a site for the making of the citizen/non-citizen distinction. But, crucially, the category of the citizen is not a homogenous one. Indeed, as Elizabeth Cohen asserts, 'citizenship does not make a citizenry equal. In fact, it appears to institutionalize both difference and inequalities, albeit in sometimes unexpected ways'.[4] Accessing welfare benefits has a stigmatising effect, dividing unproductive citizens from what Anderson refers to as the 'worker citizen', whose market participation confirms their place in the national polity.

The figure of the young, single mother – seen to stubbornly refuse the demands of sexual modernity and live a life of luxury on benefits – was a particularly potent folk devil in this period. Often, the figures of the fraudster and the asylum seeker were fused, as in an article from the *Sun* which claimed: 'We resent the scroungers, beggars and crooks who are prepared to cross every country in Europe to reach our generous benefits system.'[5] After the 2001 riots in Oldham, Burnley, and Bradford and the 9/11 attacks in the US later that year, the figure of the violent and threatening Muslim joined Britain's roll call of folk devils, with older notions of Asians as incorrigibly patriarchal becoming Islamicised, while Hindus and Sikhs were folded into the celebratory jingoism of 'Cool Britannia'.

Under New Labour's governance, 'the Muslim terrorist', the 'bogus asylum seeker' and the 'benefits scrounger' were placed in stark contrast with the increasingly acceptable figure of the white gay man. The latter was viewed as the apex of sexual modernity: socially mobile, with a disposable income and concern for appearances deemed highly compatible with New Labour's ideology of individualism and self-sufficiency. New Labour saw homophobia as an outdated stigma that prevented gays from realising their potential as full economic actors and citizens of the nation. As such, New Labour introduced legislation designed to counter this residual stigma and incentivise organising one's intimate connections into the respectable couple form. As Natalie Edwards explains, 'Their integration into the national community, in short, is worth more to the government, and to the British economy, than their exclusion'.[6] While the gay characters in *Queer as Folk* cannot be reduced to this rather flat view of gay potential, they are nonetheless shown to be flexible, economic agents whose identities are significantly undergirded by consumer goods, especially cars and mobile phones. 'The Lesbians', as they are referred to in the show, however, are another matter. Romey's 'sham' marriage to Lance appears to be motivated by solidarity and is swiftly punished in the show's moral economy. This portrayal of 'The Lesbians' as having a dangerous set of political attachments echoes the Thatcherite moral panic about the infiltration of lesbians into local government as the harbingers of the so-called 'Loony Left'.

*Queer as Folk* encapsulates the contradictory pulls of the New Labour project and hints at the racial regime produced and maintained by its Janus-faced political project. In the programme, gay men are presented as the ideal subjects of the market – as adaptable, modern individuals. For these ideal individuals to flourish, however, others must be managed, punished, or excluded. Lance needs to be banished from the moral universe for Stuart, Nathan, and Vince's world to be maintained. Lance's punishment – orchestrated by Stuart, Nathan, and Romey's jealous girlfriend but enacted by the police and border agents – places the state on the side not only of the gay community but also of the self-interested individual, unmoved by the possibility of solidarity or even a more liberal, altruistic charity. A similar fortification of the individual as the basic unit of organisation was crucial to New Labour's use of racial governance. Muslims, for example, were viewed as perversely clannish and therefore susceptible to violence and disorder, while Hindus and Sikhs were placed closer to their white counterparts in their capacity to fulfil the promise of sexual modernity. Like gay men, they were seen as ripe for assimilation into modern sexual norms.

New Labour instated a complex machinery of categorisation that reinvigorated the colonial policies of division, assimilation, punishment, and counterinsurgency to meet the needs of the 'market state'. Following the Labour Party's historic break with the trade union movement in 1995, Blair's political vision of a society in service to the market came to the fore. As Arun Kundnani summarises:

> The state's legitimacy was to be based on its role in maximising the potential of individuals to participate in the market economy. It would constantly intervene in the labour market to engineer a workforce that was fully adapted to the demands of a globalised, knowledge economy: a 'flexible' workforce with high job turnover and increasing precariousness. A cultural change in the workforce was required, embracing personal innovation, lifelong learning and adaptability.[7]

These 'constant interventions' in the labour market included designating economically unproductive behaviour 'anti-social' in order to criminalise it through highly personalised 'anti-social behaviour orders' (ASBOs) which could make it an arrestable offence to swear or play particular songs. These draconian interventions were described in the language of 'empowerment', which the state was to facilitate so that individuals could 'endure market-driven social upheaval and embrace the opportunities that markets offered'.[8] As such, the capacity and desire to be a flexible, market-oriented, innovative, entrepreneurial, and self-governing subject – an empowered individual – underpinned the forms of racial differentiation fortified by New Labour. And it was the promise of sexual modernity that would be used as the incentive to adapt to the market.

In the rest of this chapter, I'll map out the mechanisms of inclusion and exclusion, reward and punishment through which New Labour sought to create a pliable workforce, stratified and managed by race and justified by the promise of sexual modernity. Just as in the Thatcherite project, which New Labour sought to deepen and extend, the language of meritocracy offered an overarching rationale. If we read between the lines of Thatcher's claim that 'what's more desirable and more practicable than the pursuit of equality is the pursuit of equality of opportunity',[9] we can see that meritocracy is such a powerful promise precisely because it makes individuals entirely responsible for their own poverty, exclusion, or suffering. One of the innovations of Blair's approach was in articulating this vision of individual responsibility to a limited but seductive vision of sexual freedom. I'll begin with New Labour's conception of sexuality, marriage, and family, considering its use of gay rights as a particularly potent form of inclusion through which its vision for society might be realised. I'll then turn to the ways in which the promise of sexual modernity was used to discipline those deemed unable or unwilling to aspire to it, in particular South Asian Muslims and 'underclass' whites. Finally, I'll consider how socially mobile Indians, particularly Hindus, functioned as an alibi for these exclusions.

## Plastic Sexuality

*'Relationship' is these days the hottest talk of the town and ostensibly the only game in town worth playing, despite its notorious risks.*

Zygmunt Bauman, *Liquid Love*

In its first decade in power, New Labour made multiple legislative changes to bring the lives of gay people further in line with those of heterosexuals. Homosexuals were completing their transition from denizens of sexual modernity's underbelly to the embodiment of its most tantalising promise: self-realisation through the pursuit romantic love and the couple form. In 1997, New Labour began the process of equalising the age of consent for sex between men by amending the Crime and Disorder Bill. This was followed by the Sexual Offences Act 2003, which became law the following year and included removal from the statute books those sexual acts specific to the criminalisation of gay men. In 2003, the Employment Equality (Sexual Orientation) Regulations prohibited discrimination, harassment, and victimisation in the workplace on the grounds of sexual orientation, bringing homophobia in line with discrimination based on sex, religion, belief, and disability. In the same year, New Labour repealed Section 28, the Thatcherite legislation that had prohibited local authorities from 'promoting homosexuality'. In 2004, they passed the Civil Partnership Act, which granted same-sex couples access to legal partnerships that were akin to civil marriage.

These legal reforms were neither incidental to the project of New Labour, and to the racial logic nurtured under its governance, nor were they merely well-placed 'progressive' window dressing for a system of governance highly dependent on punitive and draconian security and surveillance. Rather, gay rights represented the apex of New Labour's vision of sexual modernity – and of the value of modern sexual subjects to the market state. Though civil partnerships (which paved the way for gay marriage to be brought into law in 2013) were a means of including gay people in the couple form, it is worth pausing on the timing of this inclusion. Coinciding with Britain's entry into the protracted wars in Afghanistan and Iraq, gay rights served as a means of distinguishing 'our way of life' – as progressive and civilised – from the sexual backwardness of 'Muslim' countries.

Further, this geopolitical logic dovetailed perfectly with a set of economic imperatives. While theorists of neoliberalism's break with the postwar economic settlement often focus on the Thatcher years, James Meadway observes that we might develop a more comprehensive understanding of the effects of neoliberal reforms if we examine the period of high globalisation in which neoliberal logic became hegemonic – the early 2000s.[10] As Meadway explains, 'The peak neoliberal governments – those that perfected the form – were not Thatcher and Reagan's, but those of Blair and Clinton'.[11] In this period, the welfare state was fully subordinated to the market logic of globalisation and the financial sector became the driving force of economic life. As the male breadwinner family was fully displaced by the two-income household, the disciplinary function of both the nuclear heterosexual family and the exclusion of homosexuals from this form waned. As Ben Miller asks, 'Who could look, today, at the financial capitals of London or New York and assume that homophobia is central to the function of our late-capitalist world system?'[12] New Labour's vision of the market state was one in which laziness, fecklessness, or a stubborn attachment to 'tradition' might exclude you from participation, but your sexual orientation would not.

To understand this vision, we must turn to the key intellectual figure behind New Labour: Anthony Giddens. A sociologist who was to become Blair's 'court philosopher',[13] Giddens was the academic proponent of New Labour's 'third way', which rested on the idea that – post-Cold War – ideology was over. In other words, the left/right divide was a distracting anachronism, since capitalism's victory was complete. As globalisation was inevitable, progressive politics should be organised around helping people to adapt to the market. If the nation-state and national governments were to remain relevant, their role was to facilitate global markets. The rich were 'wealth creators' and their wealth was good for everyone. Giddens recognised that capitalist development had loosened people's historic attachment to traditional family networks and the localities in which they unfolded: 'Kinship relations, it has been widely argued, have been largely destroyed with the development of modern institutions, which have left the nuclear family standing in splendid isolation'.[14] It is worth pausing on the phrasing here, given that the term 'splendid isolation' is associated with Britain's nineteenth-century diplomatic practice of avoiding permanent alliances. In his borrowing from the rhetoric of British exceptionalism, we can catch a glimpse of Giddens' larger project of cementing Britain's position within late capitalist globalisation. In many ways, Giddens is a shrewd archaeologist, but his affection for the civilization he attempts to excavate naturally contours his findings.

In his 1992 book, *The Transformation of Intimacy*, Giddens sets out a vision for what kinds of intimacy might be made possible by – and help to manage the convulsions of – a rapidly globalising world. He observes the emergence of what he refers to as 'plastic sexuality' – 'decentred sexuality, freed from the needs of reproduction'.[15] He notes that 'the creation of plastic sexuality, severed from its age-old integration with reproduction, kinship and the generations, was the precondition of the sexual revolution of the past several decades'.[16] From plastic sexuality comes not only a more comprehensive integration of women into wage labour, but the development of the couple form as the basic unit of social good. While marriage remains the model for this form, Giddens places his emphasis on personal choice and individual fulfilment rather than institutional recognition. He suggests that from plastic sexuality comes 'confluent love' – relationships chosen not for the purposes of connecting two families and their respective resources, nor for the purpose of respectability or the organisation of a household, but for intimacy, romance, and fulfilment. As relationships are chosen, they can be dissolved: 'Confluent love is active, contingent love'.[17]

According to Giddens, gays were forerunners in developing the model of confluent love, 'For they have had to "get along" without traditionally established frameworks of marriage, in conditions of relative equality between partners'.[18] He is keen to note, however, that though homosexuality might be the cutting edge, its avant-garde embrace of plastic sexuality is not the result of movements for gay liberation; rather, it issues from 'much more deep-lying, and irreversible changes than were brought about by such movements'.[19] As Giddens makes clear, these changes go much further than shifts in the meaning of sex and gender: 'what is at issue here is a basic transition in the ethics of personal life as a whole.'[20] In other words, he deftly argues that the demise of homophobia is not a moral or political victory forged by gay activism, but the realisation of the new globalised order, in which attachments must be chosen and pursued rather than taken for granted.

New Labour made this new ethics of personal life a cornerstone of its philosophy. Just as globalisation was inevitable, so too was the individuation it heralded. As Fiona Williams argued, 'A new normative family is emergent, which . . . revolves around the adult couple whose relationship is based on their parenting responsibilities, and whose priorities are rooted in work, economic self-sufficiency, education and good behaviour'.[21] While women were brought out of a purely social reproductive role and fully into the labour market, the couple form was to remain the norm, supported by legislation, precisely because it offered a way to contain intimacy and connection. Just as in the colonial context, nucleated intimacy and conjugal families were a means of staving off the chaotic possibilities of too much sexual freedom. The government's job was to make people market-ready, and confluent relationships were a suitable model through which to do this. Those who found intimacy elsewhere – in the extended family, with its capacity to rival the state's authority, or in casual, public sexual encounters – were a threat not only to sexual morality but to the economic logic through which neoliberal sexual modernity was conceived.

The raft of new legislation aimed at redressing the social and economic marginalisation of gays was a way to affirm and develop this 'adult couple' as a profound social norm. To return to the Sexual Offences Act 2003, while this reform took some homophobic laws off the statute books, it also specifically criminalised 'sexual activity in a public lavatory', or 'cottaging', which is an almost exclusively gay public sex practice. As Edwards observes, the 'criminalisation of cottaging . . . seems perfectly to illustrate New Labour's overall position on issues of equality, specifically its emphasis on reciprocal obligations and the extension of legal rights and recognitions to those willing to shoulder social and economic responsibilities'.[22] While respectable gay couples were a sign of modernity, cottaging was viewed as outdated and 'anti-social', – a key term of criminalisation in New Labour's bureaucratic vernacular – and its practitioners were to be punished.

## Exclusions

*The mud of criminalisation sticks to all those seeking refuge.*

Les Back et al.

Despite the seductive promise of conjugal intimacy, many continued to organise their lives in other ways. For those unwilling or unable to adapt to the market, exclusion was the order of the day. Hall observes that New Labour's political philosophy led to 'the remoralisation of the work ethic, and the restoration of that discredited and obscene Victorian utilitarian distinction between "the deserving" and "the undeserving" poor'.[23] Those deemed undeserving were subject to New Labour's regime of punitive state intervention, through which categories of crime proliferated dramatically. Between 2000 and 2008, 17,000 anti-social behaviour orders were issued, drawing huge numbers into the carceral state's purview. New Labour focussed their attention on an 'underclass' which they characterised as feckless and work-shy, living in dysfunctional families, unable or unwilling to embrace the promise of sexual modernity. This underclass was segmented by race, with particular habits of sexual dysfunction or backwardness associated with each racial group.

Many of New Labour's reforms emerged through the Social Exclusion Unit, set up in 1997. Supposedly established to tackle 'social exclusion', it regularly contributed to the stigmatisation, punishment, and further marginalisation of those it deemed 'at risk' of exclusion. Despite its modern rhetoric, the Social Exclusion Unit reinvigorated a racialising politics of punishment, in which poor whites were stigmatised through their unwillingness to adapt to sexual modernity and for their implicit similarity with racial Others. As we saw in the last chapter, a section of the working class have, since the end of the nineteenth century, been viewed as available for redemption through their adoption of a facsimile of bourgeois family structures. This process divided these workers from the disorderly underclass, a group excluded from the emerging category of whiteness and defined by 'idleness, licentiousness and vagrancy'[24] – precisely the qualities identified as belonging to the racialised masses in the colonies. This distinction was reinvigorated by New Labour, with this disorderly population identified as those 'at risk' of social exclusion. Though in almost all instances, the Social Exclusion Unit recognised that class was 'significant' in determining someone's marginalisation, its policy initiatives were almost universally focussed on the individual rather than on the context in which they lived, on the specific choices they made rather than on the limited options with which they were presented. In many cases, the cause of their exclusion (poverty) was taken as the effect of a more nebulous kind of marginalisation for which the individual could be blamed.

This metalepsis was particularly clear in policies on teenage pregnancy. New Labour tried to distance their approach from the 'back to basics' campaign launched under Conservative prime minister John Major which emphasised traditional family values, despite sharing the view that marriage and nuclear families were the fundamental basis of a successful society. When talking about teenage pregnancies, Tony Blair bemoaned Britain's 'shameful record', and in 1999 the government pledged to halve pregnancies for those under eighteen by mid-2010. The 1998 *Supporting Families* consultation document makes their position clear: 'Unwanted and under-age pregnancies, whether planned or unplanned, have a high personal, social and economic cost and can blight the life chances of younger teenagers.'[25] One of the contradictions at the heart of New Labour's philosophy becomes apparent here: for all the emphasis on personal choice, the only personal choices that the government actively supported were those which conformed to its model of market participation. As such, even planned and desired teenage pregnancies were viewed as a drain on society.

To counter this apparently high 'personal, social and economic cost', New Labour devised a characteristically forked approach comprising both educational and punitive initiatives, in a 'third way' defined less by compromise than by confusion. A wider rollout of sex education was the softer side of their approach, and the more punitive aspects were organised around access to benefits. The long-standing legend that young women got pregnant 'to get a council house' was elevated into an incontestable social fact and countered by removing access to council housing for young mothers. Instead, New Labour proposed to house teenaged mothers who were unable to live with their own families in semi-supervised accommodation. In essence, this was a return to mother-and-baby homes with all the social stigma still intact. The enduring myth (explored in the previous chapter) that immigration threatened to drain the welfare state of its resources was now applied specifically to 'asylum seekers'. But the language of fraud also revived fears of other kinds of 'scroungers', serving to criminalise all those who were in need of state support.

The government also set their sights on teenage fathers, with a campaign to warn them that 'sex comes with a price' and that the

Child Support Agency would pursue young men to pay child maintenance as soon as they reach working age. This focus on the 'price'
of sex runs through all of New Labour's rhetoric, research, and policy
decisions on teenage pregnancies, which views young parents exclusively through the lens of market participation. In a research project
by Karen Robson and Richard Berthoud funded by the Department
of Health, the full racial logic of this approach becomes clear: 'The
purpose of this study is to examine if and how the outcomes of early
childbearing in the UK differ by ethnic group. The main outcome
that will be examined here is whether or not a woman is in a working family, although other correlates will be examined in the
process.'[26] That the metric to be studied is so nakedly a measure of
economic productivity suggests that, from the perspective of the New
Labour government, the value of the family is determined by the
ways in which it facilitates one's labour.

According to Robson and Berthoud's research, there are distinct
patterns of family formation for each ethnic group. Pakistani and
Bangladeshi communities are viewed as adhering to the 'old-fashioned'
pattern of family formation, with early marriage and childbirth as a
norm, while Caribbean communities are placed as their polar opposite, as having chaotic domestic lives without coherent family units.
White family formation is viewed as the middle ground between
these poles. If we return to the way in which, under British colonial
rule, the idea of culture and the management of sexuality were sutured
together like a Möbius strip, we can see that this view of 'ethnic family
formation' rehearses the old colonial practices of the ethnographic
state. Here this logic is reheated into the trope of South Asians as
having 'too much culture' and Black communities 'too little', which
remained central to the maintenance and development of racial
categories under New Labour. Both 'extremes' are viewed as potentially threatening to a white bourgeois norm.

Though the research identifies young parenthood as a norm in
Pakistani and Bangladeshi communities, the moral panic around
teenage mothers focussed on single white women. According to
Berthoud and Robson, this is because these white teenagers deviated
from the norms of 'white' family formations. They thus paid a penalty

for their deviation, for their failure to inhabit the familial structures that have come to define respectable whiteness. The implications of this assessment reveal the ways in which the production of racial groups through seemingly inherent kinship structures continues into the early years of the twenty-first century. In the next sections, I'll consider how distance from sexual modernity is used to fracture South Asian communities into those who can be included in the national polity and those who are to remain on the margins.

## Community Cohesion

*The World Council of Hindus mixed class snobbery with communalism to publicly disown the Muslim rioters, hoping to make clear to whites that Hindus should not be tarnished with the same brush. Asian solidarity had died.*

Arun Kundnani

The fracturing of South Asian identity in Britain was a key shift that intensified under New Labour's rule. There has never been a homogenous British Asian community; it has always been divided geographically – as well as by religion, country of origin, migration status, gender, and language – and stratified by class. These divisions had been systematically exploited and carefully fortified through the colonial strategy of indirect rule. But in the bumpy transition from empire, when citizens of the newly independent India and Pakistan (and later, Bangladesh), still subjects of the Crown, arrived at Britain's borders, they were viewed as a largely homogenous group. As they settled and had children, this group eventually became categorised as British Asians. At the end of the 1960s and the beginning of the 1970s, the arrival of East African Asians from Kenya and Uganda drew attention to the rather more complex set of historical divisions and connections through which the categories of race were made and remade, but the meta-term of 'Asian' or 'British Asian' was still applied across the board.

While the greater social mobility and higher incomes of Indians compared to their Pakistani and Bangladeshi counterparts had been noted in earlier decades, it was in the 1990s – and specifically under New Labour – that this observation began to crystallise into a strategy of population management with an associated set of policy decisions. In the Department of Health–commissioned research quoted in the previous section, the hardening of these divisions according to the logic of sexual modernity is made explicit, stating 'Indians within the South Asian group, however, are probably more appropriately placed between the Pakistani/Bangladeshis who are exemplary of the "old fashioned" pattern, and the white pattern'.[27] By placing Indians 'closer' to white British people than their Pakistani and Bangladeshi counterparts, a racial hierarchy within the category of 'British Asian' is made an explicit mechanism of governance. This hierarchy was crucial to the racial regime that took shape under New Labour and has played an increasingly prominent role in subsequent decades.

The Islamicisation of older racial logics was already in motion when the 11 September attacks in the US took place, sharpening the category of 'Muslim' in the national imaginary. The 2001 riots in Oldham, Burnley, and Bradford had preceded 9/11 and the official shift to the War on Terror as an organising governmental paradigm, through which Muslims were targeted as distinct from other South Asians. Hot on the heels of New Labour's second successful election, these riots across northern towns from May to July set the mood for their more muted, less celebratory second term in office. A deeper look at the events in each town reveals that police harassment, state neglect, and the rise of the British National Party and other far-right nationalist groups spurred confrontations with the police, involving both white and Asian residents.

Though there had been highly organised left movements in these communities in the 1970s and 1980s, with the Asian Youth Movement and United Black Youth League in Bradford as an especially powerful political force,[28] the 2001 riots were, to borrow Kundnani's memorable phrase, 'the violence of the violated' – that it to say, 'the violence of communities fragmented by colour lines, class lines and police lines'.[29] Yet media coverage and political rhetoric portrayed the riots as acts of mindless criminality produced by innate cultural dysfunction. Though a more extensive comparison is beyond the scope of my argument, the aggressive state response to the 2001 riots functioned as the blueprint for the response to the 2011 uprisings, which were catalysed by the death at the hands of the police of a young black man named Mark Duggan in North London. In the hyperbolic media coverage focussed on masculine dysfunction, the use of 'wanted' posters, and extensive prison sentences for minor offences, the racial logic of criminalisation is consistent. As noted in the previous chapter, different groups are not racialised in isolation but in dialogue: the modes of criminalisation used against black and Muslim communities (which, of course, significantly overlap) draw from one another in both method and rhetoric.

As Yasmin Hussain and Paul Bagguley observe, 'The political and media reaction to the 2001 riots finally fixed into the national consciousness an image of young South Asian Muslim men as the new "enemy within" – an image subsequently reinforced by political reactions to 9/11 and 7/7'.[30] If we focus on the Bradford uprisings, it's clear that these events marked a crucial intensification of New Labour's highly punitive approach to any form of 'anti-social behaviour'. Ninety per cent of those charged were convicted – much higher than the usual rate of conviction for such offences – and lengthy custodial sentences were handed down to people with no previous criminal record. Hussain and Bagguley's research confirms that both the political elite (including David Blunkett, the Home Secretary at the time) and the criminalised community viewed these harsh sentences as a kind of collective punishment, designed to teach Bradford's Pakistani Muslim community a lesson.

Just as significant as the draconian prison sentences, however, was the method through which the rioters were found and charged. 'Wanted' posters appeared in local press and were put up across Bradford – in schools, mosques, and community centres. While many white people were involved in the Bradford riots, their images did not appear on these posters, and their places of work, worship, and education were not targeted. Police information reporting phone lines were set up in English and Urdu to encourage people to turn in their neighbours and families. This approach was an explicit attempt to shame the community into informing on its brothers, fathers, and sons. In an attempt to spare their families the humiliation and indignity of raids and arrests – familiar to many working-class communities with direct experience of immigration enforcement and policing tactics – many young men turned themselves in, expecting to act as witnesses or receive fines for their minimal participation or mere presence, rather than years of incarceration. This approach traded on the notion that Islam forms a culture organised around shame and honour, though one could just as easily argue that any stigmatised social group might have responded in precisely the same fashion if subjected to the same regime of collective punishment.

Following the riots, the government commissioned several reports, the most influential of which was the Cantle report. According to Ted Cantle, the riots were the result of ethnic segregation, cultural insularity, and a lack of national values to which racialised communities were obliged to subscribe. Cantle focusses on the absence of social and institutional spaces in which white and South Asian residents regularly interact. As Kundnani notes, however, 'The segregation of communities, the roots of which lay in institutional racism, came to be perceived as "self-segregation" – an attempt by Asians to create their own exclusive areas or "no-go areas" because they did not want to mix with whites'.[31] As Kundnani elaborates, this metalepsis by which effect is read as cause amounts to a self-fulfilling prophecy. In the Cantle report – and in Home Secretary David Blunkett's rhetoric – Muslim communities not speaking English at home was the focus of special attention.

This focus on the home space of British Muslims dovetails with many of New Labour's other concerns. Like the teenage mother and the benefits scrounger, it was through non-criminal behaviour taking place in the domestic sphere that Muslim criminality was assumed. While Muslims may have been seen as having a different kind of disreputable home life from the other prominent folk devils – with too much family and too much culture rather than too little of both; with too strong a set of social bonds rather than too weak – they were equally defined through their distance from sexual modernity. The Cantle report, with its focus on the domestic life and gender relations of Muslims, became the blueprint for subsequent government interventions. The 2016 Casey Review, commissioned by the Conservative government, rehearses this focus on the kinship structures of Pakistani and Bangladeshi Muslims, quoting right-wing ideologue David Goodheart's claim that transnational marriage practices were creating a 'first generation in every generation', thereby preventing the proper integration of Muslim communities. As the authors of the report claim, 'We were told in a review visit that in one northern town all except one of the Councillors of Asian ethnicity (all men) had married a wife from Pakistan'. This detail serves to discredit Muslim political participation via the implicit accusation of dubious domestic and sexual arrangements.

The singling out of Muslims for this agenda is crucial to the development of a racial regime in which the category of Asian is fully broken up and divided into assimilable and non-assimilable parts. As Bagguley and Hussain summarise:

> Whilst previously the concern was to define ethnicity in this context in terms of supposedly traditional, fixed and internally homogenous collectivities based upon the national origins of the initial migrants, this has now shifted to focus upon religion as the defining characteristic. In particular Muslims are now seen as the most problematic group, and the ones who are reluctant to assimilate, the most deprived and the most dangerous.[32]

The dividing up of the old category of Asian also made it possible to reimagine 'Muslim' as a multiethnic racial category. Muslims from around the world had settled in Britain for centuries, with South Asian lascars working for the East India Company, Yemeni migrants arriving after the opening of the Suez Canal in 1869, and Muslims from Algeria, Turkey, Palestine, Morocco, Egypt, Somalia, Nigeria, and many other countries making homes in Britain in the postwar period. In the 1990s and early 2000s, many Muslim refugees arrived from Bosnia-Herzegovina and Kosovo. Further, as the wars in Afghanistan and Iraq progressed, refugees displaced by these conflicts began to arrive on the shores of Britain, the imperial power whose interventions had led to their displacement. And, of course, over Britain's long colonial history, it competed (and collaborated) with the Ottoman and Mughal empires.

The changing patterns of settlement, Britain's continued involvement in military intervention and occupation in Muslim-majority countries, and the renewed construction of a global Muslim identity worked together to reconstruct the category of 'Muslim'. Though this marked a huge shift in how race functions in Britain, it did not overturn other racial categories. Rather, it allowed for multiple modalities of exclusion and inclusion to work together. This multiplicity is part of what gives race its slickness, its resistance to being exposed as a complex social fiction. The revival of Muslims as a racial category was not only a matter of rhetoric but of policy; the War on Terror targeted mosques, community centres, and Muslim youth groups as sites of surveillance, infiltration, and criminalisation that impacted people regardless of their heritage or country of origin. While this targeting did not seal the internal fractures and divergences within British Muslim life – which continues to be organised along class, regional, ethnic, and national, as well as political and sectarian, lines – it did serve to cohere Muslims as a group in the public imaginary. Here we can see that racism produces race – even if it does so via the alibi of culture, nation, or religion.

## Meritocracy

*Meritocracy: a hegemonic language for the ruling class.*

Richard Seymour

In his 2006 satirical novel *Tourism*, British Asian writer Nirpal Singh Dhaliwal points to this imbrication of British Indians, particularly Hindus, with New Labour. He describes Margaret Thatcher as 'Britain's first Indian Prime Minister' and suggests that, in their embrace of Thatcherite policies but with a new emphasis on social progress, the New Labour project marked an offer of 'Thatcherism without racial prejudice' aimed at securing the support of Indians in Britain.[33]

This view, however sardonically expressed, gestures towards the under-theorised position of Indians in the political ecology of New Labour. However, it leaves out the ways in which the inclusion of Indians did not mark the end of racism but a reformulation of Britain's racial regime – one that would ultimately strengthen rather than dissolve the power of racial thinking. As poet Jay Bernard notes, exceptions are a potent tool of racial logic: 'power is never total: it relies on exceptions, the same way you can put holes in a metal beam to make it stronger'.[34] The assimilation of upwardly mobile Indians fractured the category of British Asian but fortified the system of racial govern-ance using a logic that would be finessed by subsequent Tory governments in the twenty-first century. Further, this image of the upwardly mobile, successful, aspirational Indian acted as evidence of the meritocracy New Labour claimed to promote. Of course, as Seymour implies in the epigraph for this section, the language of meritocracy is used to justify rather than ameliorate poverty and marginalisation, placing the responsibility for one's limited life choices on the individual rather than the context in which they live.

While many South Asian Muslims found themselves at the sharp end of the twinned policies of assimilation and exclusion, British Hindus were increasingly welcomed into the national polity. At the end of the 1990s, British Asian youth culture gained an increasingly large platform. In a moment dubbed 'Asian cool', music by Talvin Singh and Nitin Sawhney hit the charts, the sketch comedy *Goodness Gracious Me* found huge popularity on BBC2, and the character of Anna appeared on hit television show *This Life*. Anna is a particularly significant example, as it was rare before this time to see an Asian woman character who shared the concerns of her white counterparts: Anna drank, smoked, worked as a lawyer, and had various romantic escapades. As Kundnani observes, alongside the new visibility in television and music, 'Asian millionaires were fêted by leading poli-ticians and glamourised in the media', producing 'the closest thing that Britain had to the American 'rags-to-riches' immigrant dream'.[35] While these developments were marketed as 'Asian cool', the major-ity of the artists, writers, and actors were Sikhs or Hindus, with Muslims relatively underrepresented, and the focus was on London rather than on the British Asian experience in Birmingham, Bradford, or Leicester.

This cultural dominance was the outcome of class disparities, with Pakistani and Bangladeshi communities among the most deprived in the country, while Indians had levels of income and education comparable with (and sometimes outstripping) their white counterparts. The reasons for these disparities are manifold, but one of the most significant can be found in the kinds of work available to these different groups upon their arrival. While many Indians who migrated in the immediate postwar period were from middle-class backgrounds, the majority of Pakistani arrivals the following decade left the highly militarised and deprived region of Azad Kashmir following the construction of the Mangla Dam in the 1960s, which decimated the region and left hundreds of villages under water. They were recruited to work the night shift across mill towns in the north of England, and they were strategically segregated from white workers in order to maintain labour discipline. Bangladeshi arrivals to Britain were largely from Sylhet and migrated following the 1971 war, which led to a second partition of the subcontinent. Though the land disputes and military conflicts which prompted people to leave South Asia are very easily traced back to the British Empire, these class disparities are consistently viewed as cultural rather than issuing from specific economic, geopolitical, and military circumstances.

The reheated colonial culturalism was a highly effective means of justifying New Labour's continuation of Thatcherite methods of governance. As Angela McRobbie suggests, forms of gender- and race-aware governmentality became built into educational reform.[36] New Labour was quick to proclaim (in the same manner as Thatcher, twenty years before) that its policies had created a meritocratic society in which class politics, feminism, and antiracism could only be anachronistic. Within this putative meritocracy, British Indians have been characterised as aspirational, with entrepreneurship and 'hard work' posited as universal characteristics either inherent to the group or as contextually logical responses to conditions of marginalisation. The figure of the hardworking Indian remains culturally intelligible and politically useful within what McRobbie refers to as 'new integrationism', which she suggests has the 'post 9/11 ring of the contemporary'. It is a discourse in which 'the visibility of Black and Asian people . . . within the talent-led economy would ideally replace the need for arguments about institutionalised racism'.[37]

Sexuality, gender, and kinship practices are at the heart of this culturalist logic. In keeping with the approach of the Cantle report (which he commissioned), then-home secretary David Blunkett publicly denounced 'forced marriages' and 'female circumcision' and insisted that South Asian communities should organise arranged marriages only between brides and grooms already resident in the UK. Speaking to 'the leaders of the Asian Muslim community', MP Ann Cryer told them to 'encourage their people to put their daughters' happiness, welfare and human rights first. If they do, their communities will progress and prosper, in line with the Sikh and Hindu communities'.[38] Though arranged marriages are common across all three religions, when politically expedient to view Sikhs and Hindus as subjects of sexual modernity who might embrace plastic sexuality and confluent love, this commonality is obscured or ignored. Like gay men, British Hindus and Sikhs were viewed as economically productive citizens – ripe for assimilation into sexual modernity – whose participation in the market state was evidence of its inclusive, meritocratic nature.

At the start of the 2020s, there were more black and brown faces among the political elite than ever before, including several prominent British Asians. As chancellor, Rishi Sunak was responsible for accelerating the Covid-19 pandemic's second wave with his public subsidy for private catering businesses. After holding this position, he became prime minister in 2022. As home secretary, Priti Patel presided over one of the most violent, expulsive, and militarised border regimes in Europe. In the same role, Suella Braverman claimed that seeing a flight take asylum seekers to Rwanda is her 'dream' and 'obsession'.[39] These high-profile figures offer a highly effective alibi against not only the charge of racism, but its very existence. Sajid Javid tweets about 'sick Asian paedophiles', Kemi Badenoch insists she doesn't 'care about colonialism' and that 'critical race theory' is an enemy of equality; and Shaun Bailey, Conservative mayoral candidate, proclaims that his mother's insistence that he spend as little time in the black community as possible was the secret to his success. These prominent figures present themselves as incontrovertible evidence of merit-ocracy. While the strategy of inclusion can, as I show in this book, be traced back to indirect rule as a technique of imperial governance, New Labour reinvigorated this strategy, redividing British Asian communities into discrete groups and offering the powerful logic of sexual modernity as an alibi for entrenching racial hierarchy.

# 6

## Identity Crisis

### Mimic Men

*I swayed on the spot, psyching myself up for what was to come: the switch
from West to East, South to North, English to Punjabi, rationality to
superstition, smoked almonds to salted peanuts.*

Sathnam Sanghera, The Boy with the Topknot

As the illusory egalitarianism of New Labour gave way to the brute
reality of racial exclusion, protracted and bloody wars in Iraq and
Afghanistan, and the upward redistribution of wealth, a series of
novels and memoirs by British Asian men were published to significant popular and critical acclaim. These books were all organised
around a trope that one might have expected to have been long since
discarded as passé: the 'identity crisis'. The first of these texts was
Nirpal Singh Dhaliwal's aforementioned novel *Tourism*, which follows
the adventures of a young man from Southall who traverses the city
to trade on his 'exoticism' and has affairs with wealthy, fatuous white
women. *Tourism* was followed in 2007 by Sarfraz Manzoor's *Greetings
from Bury Park* (later adapted for the screen), a memoir of negotiat-
ing life as a British Asian man living in Luton and centred on his
relationship with his family and his obsession with Bruce Spring-
steen.[1] Then came *The Boy with the Topknot* (originally published in
2008 as *If You Don't Know Me By Now*), a memoir by Sathnam
Sanghera that explores the discovery of his father and sister's schiz-
ophrenia as well as his attempt to 'come out' to his mother about his
desire to date white women.[2] Sanghera followed this memoir with a

novel, *Marriage Material*, a rewriting of Arnold Bennett's *The Old Wives Tale* relocated to a Wolverhampton corner shop.[3] Each of these books spin familiar yarns of overbearing mothers and absent fathers, of desire for national belonging, of young men trapped between suffocating traditions and the tantalising promise of freedom.

These books are significant partly for their volume and similarity; you could take a sentence from one and seamlessly insert it into any other. The fact of their publication in quick succession between 2006 and 2013 suggests that there was a ready market for stories of British Asian masculinity, particularly narratives of assimilation into sexual modernity. Each of the texts follows a British Asian man (Sikhs, Hindus, and Muslims are all represented) who views himself as a fugitive from the strictures of Asian 'culture' with its uniquely repressive and controlling sexual mores. The central drama of these texts is found in the attempt by the protagonists to 'break free' from their family and culture to establish themselves as distinct individuals, able to capitalise on the promise of sexual modernity by marrying white women and getting jobs in the media. These are narratives about accessing the market – both economic and sexual – as the primary mechanism of self-realisation. After they have made a sufficient break with their stultifying traditions, they are able to find a more limited rapprochement with their families, incorporating some small element of their 'culture' back into their sense of self.

Despite the seemingly upbeat formula that underpins these narratives of individual self-fashioning, the men's stories are fraught with anxiety about the 'truth' of identity and the difficulties in establishing themselves as properly modern subjects. As such, they seek urgently to distance themselves from the violent figures – the folk devils of the gang member, the terrorist, the groomer – that we'll encounter in this chapter. We might think of controversial Trinidadian novelist (of South Asian origin) V. S. Naipaul's 'Mimic Men' as a precursor to this agitated wrangling with South Asian masculinity. They share with Naipaul a similar conception of South Asian cultures as stagnant pools, with arranged marriages and extended family structures forming the central planks of social life – in stark comparison to the tide of modernity represented by Europe. In these texts, arranged marriage is understood as fundamentally repressive, with its opposite, love marriage (essentially Giddens's 'confluent love') assumed to be universal and natural.

These narratives share the basic structure of a 'coming out' story which, as Esther Saxey notes, 'are not a by-product of the process of becoming lesbian, gay or bisexual, but a contribution to the work of creating such identities'.[4] Though ostensibly a genre specific to queer life, coming out stories necessarily circumscribe the narrative resources for heterosexuals too. In these memoirs, the protagonist knows he is different in some crucial way from his family and community; he locates this difference in his commitment to a set of modern values and aesthetics that he associates with whiteness. Through this commitment, he can transcend the 'culture clash', resolve his identity crisis, and assert the freedom to be his 'authentic self'. This claim to freedom becomes a kind of incantation. Sanghera repeatedly states his commitment to individualism: 'you have to live with the person you love; individual happiness is everything; you can't live your life for other people'.[5] In these narratives, the choice of sexual partner, rather than something more expansive, is viewed as the epitome of freedom. For these writers, as per New Labour, the gay subject is the vanguard of sexual modernity. By cleaving their stories to the model of 'coming out', they can establish themselves as properly modern in contrast to their recalcitrant families and cultures.

These books underscore the centrality of masculinity, heterosexuality, and marriage to sexual modernity's conception of the good life. They find in these structures a route to authentic selfhood and self-realisation: the hallmarks of sexual modernity's constrained but compelling vision of freedom. Individualism is cultivated in these texts as a moral or political good in and of itself, grounded in a vision of liberty based on consumerist choice – these books are littered with references to brand names and anxious displays of cultural capital. The Asian family is characterised as producing a dysfunctional masculinity, so the market, both sexual and labour, becomes the route to masculine self-realisation. The apparent dynamism of consumerist self-making is particularly seductive for these writers, and they draw on the dominant discourse of selfhood in which sexuality is foundational. Yet the texts betray little interest in the erotic. Rather, their investment is in romantic love, ending in marriage, with a partner of their own choosing. As Sanghera summarises, 'I don't want to live a partial life. I want to make the most of the freedoms I've been granted and I want to end up with someone who wants to be with me for what I am'.[6] In this chapter, I'll reveal the animating presence of the 'culture clash' in Britain's racial regime. As we'll see, the colonial fascination with South Asian masculinity invigorates contemporary cultures of racism, now aimed squarely at Muslim men, whose threatening presence is used to justify the expansion of racial violence in the form of state surveillance, incarceration, and deportation.

## Historicising the Culture Clash

*When he said he was Pakistani, I declared I was British.*

Sarfraz Manzoor, *Greetings from Bury Park*

The idea of an identity crisis does profound ideological work to prop up the racial regime of contemporary Britain. It rests on the idea that the children of immigrants (and their children, and their children, and their children) are caught between the traditional culture of their parents and the freedoms offered in Britain. Though sexuality is not always referenced directly in this discourse, it functions as its implicit, invigorating source. Prior to the War on Terror, the fracturing of the category of British Asian and the new prominence of Muslim men in the national imaginary could be traced to two key events: the Satanic Verses controversy (commonly known as the Rushdie affair) in 1988 and the 2001 riots discussed in the previous chapter. These were key moments in the calcification of the category of 'British Asian' into distinct religious communities. While Sikhs, Hindus, and Asian Christians were expected to resolve their 'identity crisis' through assimilation, it was assumed that Muslim men would be more likely to turn to violence.

The Rushdie affair was an important moment in the development of contemporary Islamophobia, a fulcrum to turn religion into a key fault line, dividing the Asian community into threatening and unthreatening in the national imaginary. *The Satanic Verses* caused some controversy for its irreverent depiction of the prophet Muhammad. Images of young British Asian men burning books – the illiberal act *par excellence* – circulated alongside similar images from Iran, India, and further afield. The diplomatic crisis between Britain and Iran that ensued was taken as disturbing evidence of the reach and power of Muslim networks globally.

The response to the protests from Thatcher's government is worth pausing on here, as it is suggestive of the ways in which the idea of a 'culture clash' is made in the continuities and ruptures between colonial and postcolonial governance. In 1989, Home Secretary Douglas Hurd made a speech at a gathering of Muslim leaders that emphasised the importance of proper national integration for ethnic minorities, the need to learn about British culture without abandoning one's own faith, and the necessity of refraining from violence. His deputy, John Patten, followed this up with an open letter to Muslim community leaders and then, two weeks later, an article entitled 'On Being British'. As we've seen, the idea of community leaders who can mediate on matters of culture and religion – now so entrenched that it feels like common sense – has its roots in the practice of indirect rule through which the British Empire sought to enlist local elites in service of the imperial project.

Patten's letter anticipates David Cameron's 'muscular liberalism' (to which I'll return at the end of the chapter) in which it is not enough to follow the laws of the land. Rather, citizenship is rendered a question of belonging rather than bureaucracy, and the terms of belonging are set by the state. Patten uses a similarly paternalistic tone to Cameron, beginning his letter, 'The Government understands how much hurt and anxiety that book has caused, and we also understand that insults, particularly to a deeply held faith, are not easily forgotten or forgiven'.[7] As Talal Asad observes, 'Here surely is the atavistic voice of an English colonial governor responding kindly to the injured sensibilities of his native subjects'.[8] The letter and subsequent directive on national identity sets up some of the interventions that have followed: it offers assurances that no one expects

Muslims to 'give up' their beliefs or traditions but qualifies this assurance with a set of 'obligations': that Muslims speak English, learn about democracy, and observe tolerance.

While these instructions now seem rather banal, they are an early and pivotal example of the ways in which the British state attempts to regulate not only the actions but the *identities* of its citizens. To paraphrase Stoler, the state is concerned with educating our desires – how we think, what we feel, to whom or what we are attached. As Asad argues, the Rushdie affair was a threat not to the power of the British government (which was not at all imperilled by a few small protests, however shocking they may have appeared) but to its authority: 'The frightening thing about the Rushdie affair for the British liberal elite is the existence of political activity by a small population that seeks authority for its difference in its own historical, religious traditions'.[9] That some British citizens may find their social, spiritual, and cultural centre of gravity outside of the promise of sexual modernity persists as a source of racial anxiety, fuelling nationalist convulsions.

If the Rushdie affair inaugurated a new set of fault lines around religion, the Cantle report in 2001, discussed in the previous chapter, relocated these fault lines within individuals, producing the now-familiar story of a clash of cultures. This framing became dominant so quickly that the Channel 4 documentary on the riots televised in 2002 was called *Culture Clash*. Mediatised images of street clashes between South Asian and white men ensured that these events were seen through the prism of race rather than poverty, poor housing, or unemployment.[10] Though the official report noted these conditions of marginalisation, it quickly sidelined material realities in favour of grave warnings that young British Pakistanis were living 'parallel lives' to their white counterparts. The constant repetition of this rhetoric fortifies the notion that Muslim communities are self-segregating and recalcitrant and that young people can only escape these oppressive values if they embrace the freedoms of sexual modernity. Until they do so, they will be trapped within a 'culture clash' that leads to violence. The report also made references to the ways in which the 'burden of "back home" politics' – by which it appeared to mean the politics of South Asia – retained an influence over political matters in the metropole. In this fear of 'back home', we hear an echo of the ways in which the Rushdie affair drew the British state's concerned attention to the global currents of Muslim life.

'Identity crisis', 'parallel lives', and 'culture clash' are all what Barbara and Karen Fields refer to as the 'ordinary turns of phrase that derail thought',[11] with these terms circulating as common sense. Indeed, it is not uncommon to hear British Asians talk about themselves in precisely this idiom: there is a thriving industry to promote and support this story, hence the spate of 'culture clash' memoirs in the 2000s. Yet the notion of a 'clash' obscures the prosaic reality of syncretic and dynamic cultures, of the 'convivial' connections forged in everyday life.[12] Further, while it might seem to be a benign or irrelevant trope, the notion of an identity crisis underpins the idea of a universal self that a surfeit of tradition, 'culture', or family might threaten to distort or overwhelm. This distortion of the self is viewed as dangerous for both individuals and the national polity. As such, the nation-state becomes the protector of the self, there to coax, cajole, or coerce us away from the strictures of culture or tradition and into the light of individualism.

## Colonial Masculinity and Counterinsurgency

*[Punjabis are] good at drinking . . . and fighting. Sometimes spin bowling.*
                                                    Nirpal Singh Dhaliwal, *Tourism*

The construction of Asian men within Britain's racial regime can be better understood if we examine the legacy of colonial fascination with South Asian masculinity. As we have seen, imperial domination was achieved through processes of gendering colonial subjects, and these ideas form the unacknowledged basis for contemporary understandings of gender and race. While the expectations of manliness, self-restraint, and competence attached to bourgeois white masculinity were forged in dialogue with the gendered habits of colonised subjects, these interconnections are obscured. As Virinder Kalra notes, 'In the shift from colonial to postcolonial, mundane forms of governance induce a sense of amnesia'.[13] As such, the figures I describe in the next section are assumed to arrive fully formed on the shores of the mainland in the postwar period, strangers anew despite long imperial intimacies.

The characterisation of British Asian men as improperly gendered – whether hyper-masculine or emasculated[14] – has its basis in imperial racial taxonomies. Natives were not viewed as a homogenous mass, but as a series of distinct groups. Sikhs, for example, were considered a 'martial race' – defined by strength, bravery, and loyalty. However, these characteristics did not make them equal to their white counterparts: instead 'their portrayal was like that of a "buffalo", stolid masculinity, rather than something of equivalence to the European norm'.[15] As such, the broader racial taxonomy of the British empire had a global scope. It identified Sikhs and Gurkhas as 'martial races', placing them in the same category as, for example, Scottish Highlanders. This designation was not merely rhetorical – it had real material consequences: the 'martial races' were recruited into the imperial army, thus producing the very military masculinity deemed inherent.

In contrast to Sikhs, however, the Pathans in the North-West Frontier – though also viewed as a 'martial race' – were seen to embody a more subversive masculinity, as the North-West Frontier remained resistant to colonial control. Drawing on older narratives of homosexuality as a distinct Oriental practice, the British believed that sodomy was rife in the region. In his notorious essay on pederasty, arch Orientalist Richard Burton identifies the Punjab, Sind, and Kashmir as within the 'Sotadic Zone', in which sodomy is 'popular and endemic'. The myth of Pathan homosexuality taken up by the British military did not necessarily render them feminine in the febrile British sexual imagination. Instead, they were understood to embody a distinct, unrestrained masculinity. This longstanding association between 'Eastern' masculinities (particularly Muslim men) and homosexuality persists in the trope of the closeted 'Islamist terrorist' described in the next section.

If Pathans were viewed as homosocial, subversive, and dangerously virile – the forerunner of the Asian gang or Islamist terrorist – the babu figure acted as the blueprint for the model minority, defined by 'passivity, squareness, weakness and weirdness'.[16] The term 'babu' was initially applied to Western-educated, bourgeois Bengalis, who were constructed in the colonial imaginary as the polar opposite of the manly Englishman. This emasculated character was summed up in Thomas Macaulay's sneering description: 'The physical organiza-tion of the Bengalee [sic] is feeble even to effeminacy. He lives in a constant vapour bath. His pursuits are sedentary, his limbs delicate, his movements languid. During many ages he has been trampled upon by men of bolder and more hardy breeds'.[17] Just as the view of Punjabis as brave if somewhat foolhardy acted as an alibi for their preferential recruitment into the military, so too did the view of Bengalis as feeble and bookish offer justification for their recruitment into the colonial civil service.

As Mrinalini Sinha observes,

> It was the shift in British colonial attitudes towards Western-educated Indians, from mediators between the colonial administration and the rest of the Indian population to an unrepresentative and artificial minority representing nothing but the anomalies of their own situation, that was signalled by the late nineteenth-century concept of the 'effeminate *babu*'.[18]

This notion that the Bengali is 'fitted by habit for a foreign yoke' was particularly crucial to British attempts to dismiss the burgeoning Indian nationalist movement (in which middle class Bengalis were particularly prominent) as the domain of a weak, indulgent kind of man, unrepresentative of the wider population. Further, in the eugen-icist language of 'breeds' and the Darwinian description of physical and psychological weakness, we can identify the brutal implications of race as the justificatory logic of colonial exploitation.

With caste, region, and religion fixed in the colonial imaginary, they were unable to understand the subject population in any other terms. As such, when the British encountered 'thuggee' – essentially groups of bandits who robbed and murdered travellers or pilgrims – they conceived of this as the inherent character of a distinct caste of hereditary criminals. It is difficult to ascertain the full picture of 'thuggee': as Kim Wagner's work shows, 'the only sources available to historians examining the "Thugs" of early nineteenth-century India are those produced by the very authorities who persecuted them'.[19] Nonetheless, records show that this was a practice carried out by a diverse range of men from a variety of backgrounds. Though groups offered some divine justification for robbing and murdering through offerings to Kali, this was an essentially economic arrangement rather than the religious fanaticism it was portrayed as by British authorities.

As Wagner observes, the 'thugs' have been taken up as the forerunners of modern 'religious' terrorists, with counterinsurgency scholar David C. Rapoport asserting, 'The Thugs murdered more than any known terrorist group'.[20] This idiosyncratic genealogy – assembled with little in the way of evidence – can only make sense if we understand the ways in which imperial racial taxonomies continue to inform (though never fully determine) the practices of race-making today. Just as in the colonial context, in which the identification of 'thugs' as a criminal caste justified indefinite detention and extralegal judiciary intervention, the War on Terror justifies the suspension of civil liberties and legal process by turning 'terrorist' into an ontological category – one that all Muslims are imagined to potentially embody.

These various categories of native masculinity continue to shape the racial regime that dominates life in Britain. But though there is tremendous continuity, both the archetypes and the methods of domination evolve to meet a contradictory and shifting set of political and economic demands. To give an example, while 'thuggee' was understood as the inherent practice of a kind of fanatical Hindu lower caste, these associations of hereditary violence are now ascribed to young Muslim men in Britain. Further, as Kalra notes, ascriptions of gendered status are not always coherent:

> The treatment of early Asian male migrants in the cotton mills of the North West of England can be read through one set of representations that viewed Asians as preferable employees because

they were seen to have nimble fingers, as children and women
before them in the mills, emphasising a continuity with the effeminate and infantile [. . .] Alternatively, their contact with white
women on the mill floor was restricted because of what was perceived as a sexual attraction associated with 'dark, handsome
strangers'. Both of these views of masculinity were mobilized to
restrict the male workers to the night shift.[21]

Race is made and remade in specific circumstances. The norms of
bourgeois respectable masculinity – against which racial Others are
measured – also evolve; while the manly Englishman of the nineteenth century would revile homosexuality, for example, today too
violent an expression of homophobia is highly suspect. The continuities between imperial governance and the making of an exclusionary
national polity cannot be located only in a set of representations but
in the modes of governance which mobilise – and sometimes bring
into being – the looming threat of the perverse other.

## Folk Devils

*I looked at myself in the mirror, tracing the ethnicities in my face: thick
Eurasian eyebrows; a round Tatar face; fine black oriental hair; a
Mediterranean nose; full Indic lips and wide Asiatic eyes.*

Nirpal Singh Dhaliwal, *Tourism*

While the characters of the babu and the thug have receded, new
figures of terror and abjection, dwelling in the shadows of sexual
modernity, animate Britain's racial regime. By figures, I don't mean
stereotypes; rather, figures are something closer to myths, sharing
the same haunting structure of the primordial, rather than merely
the expected or clichéd. As Puar notes, these figures are often surreal,
composite, and sexually charged. She lists 'the (female) suicide
bomber, the burqa'ed figure (female? male passing for female?), the
monstrous terrorist-fag, the activist crushed by a bulldozer in Palestine, the Iraqi civilians brutally tortured by American soldiers in Abu

Ghraib, the oddly charismatic (sexy, even?) Osama bin Laden'.[22] These figures are made monstrous by their distance from respectable bourgeois gender norms – the women are threateningly masculine; the men perversely feminine. In the British context, the 'homegrown terrorist', the 'Asian gang', and the 'child groomer' epitomise sexual and gender dysfunction. They all take shape in relation to a model of Asians as defined by an unchanging culture, in which overbearing mothers and absent fathers produce an excess of tradition and a lack of individualism, leading to a dangerous moral deficiency.

The 7/7 attacks – a series of suicide bombings on tubes and buses in London that left fifty-two dead in July 2005 – gave a new shape to the fear of these figures. Further, many of the bombers were revealed to be British, from Leeds, Luton, and Bradford, bringing the figure of the homegrown terrorist into the popular imagination. Counterintuitively, this figure is assumed to be highly emasculated. His act of violence is viewed as the result of a deep and abiding lack: a lack of suitable male role models, a lack of economic or social prospects, a lack of heterosexual potential. The idea that the suicide bomber might be a closet homosexual circulates widely, albeit in coded ways. In the film *My Brother the Devil*, for example, to obscure the fact that his brother is gay, Mo tells his friends his brother's 'secret' is that he's involved with a militant Islamic group.[23] A similar plot line appears in an episode of American legal drama *The Good Wife*. This trope emerges from the assumption that the apparently repressive force of Islamic sexual customs is a cover for the unique sexual deviance of Muslim men, who have been characterised as homosexual in the Orientalist imaginary for several centuries. As Joseph Boone observes, by 1780 this trope was so well established that Jeremy Bentham asserted it as an ancient fact: 'Even now, wherever the Mahometan religion prevails, such practices seem to be attended with but little dispute'.[24] The more recent idea of a 'double life' adds another powerful dimension to the enduring notion of Muslim homosexuality by articulating the metaphor of the closet from gay life to the 'secret' of a violent political plot.

In a lineup of recent folk devils, the Asian gang can be found alongside the Islamic fundamentalist. As Claire Alexander notes, the idea of the Asian gang gained currency in the 1990s, bringing together a potent mix of fears around urban criminality, underclass poverty, and, following the Rushdie affair, religious fundamentalism. The gang is already a racialised trope, predominantly associated with black men, and the Asian gang 'also carries its own culturally specific twists – of culture conflict, religious antipathy, of alienness and unknowability, of introspective, intra-ethnic hatred'.[25] The notion of an unchanging diasporic culture, imported wholesale from a home-land held outside of historical time, becomes one half of the culture clash model. As Wendy Brown notes, while the West is assumed to 'have' culture, others are assumed to 'be' culture.[26] In the Asian gang's construction, we can hear an echo of the colonial moral panic over 'Thuggee'. The discourse on gangs posits that violence stems from a collective defined by mindless loyalty rather than the rational, sanc-tioned, and legible connections of romantic love or the nuclear family. In this way, the gang shares a poetics with the racially charged myth of the extended family or religious community. Both the extended family and the gang are subject to suspicion because they are ways in which people organise social reproduction outside of the nuclear family structure. As such, they appear not only distinct from the structures of national belonging but also resistant to capture or regulation by the state.

The most recent addition to this list of folk devils is the 'grooming gang'. Since the 2010s, the organised sexual exploitation of young women and girls has been consistently in the headlines. There have been a series of high-profile convictions of groups of men found guilty of crimes relating to child sexual exploitation, and many of those involved have been of British Pakistani men. While the sexual impli-cations of the 'gang' and the 'terrorist' are less prominent, the sexual takes centre stage in the moral panic about 'grooming gangs'. I borrow the conceit of the moral panic from Stuart Hall et al.'s *Policing the Crisis*, in which they argue that the public obsession with 'mugging' in the 1970s condensed a series of political crises into a simple, singular trope: that of the black mugger. High unemployment, unrest in Northern Ireland, and the wider social fractures wrought by economic crisis were displaced onto this folk devil, despite the fact that 'mugging' was neither a defined criminal offence nor a new or growing phenomenon.[27] More recently, Barnaby Raine has taken up the framework of the moral panic to theorise anti-Semitism, particularly in the wake of the accusations levelled at the Labour Party under the leadership of Jeremy Corbyn. According to Raine, a moral panic refers to a real set of events (anti-Semitism, street robbery, and sexual exploitation all do happen) and the paranoid reaction to these events (widespread media coverage and commentary, a sense of crisis, changes to law or policy on the basis of the assumed threat). Crucially, both the real events and the paranoid reaction can be traced to the same source.

The moral panic surrounding grooming gangs draws our attention to the ways in which nationalism can narrate the consequences of state neglect to shore up racial divisions. In the case of 'grooming gangs', organised sexual abuse did take place, on a significant scale, and many of the perpetrators were Muslim. The notion of a 'gang', however, separates these cases from other examples of organised sexual violence, such as in the Catholic Church. Organised sexual exploitation largely took place in deindustrialised towns. As formal, unionised, or simply consistent economic opportunities receded, along with local services and functioning high streets, the nighttime economy, in the form of taxis and takeaways, played a disproportionate economic and social role. Asian men were concentrated in these service jobs, giving them social power on a terrain that had been radically disorganised by the demise of industry. While social services, the police, the Crown Prosecution Service, and children's services were aware of organised sexual exploitation, there is ample evidence that state services were dismissive of the victims, viewing them as feckless, chaotic, and highly sexualised women engaging in voluntary relationships or sex work with significantly older men.[28] The victims were viewed as failing to self-realise, as engaging in the 'wrong' sexual economies, as turning away from the promise of sexual modernity. It is notable, then, that it is only when these girls are narrated as symbols of the nation that their suffering is given any credence.

The narrative which took shape through sustained coverage in the right-wing media, as well as by far-right groups such as the

English Defence League (who used these cases of sexual violence to rebuild their base), told a particular, racialised story about this abuse. According to this narrative, Muslim men target white girls as 'easy prey' (unlike women from their own cultural community, whose 'honour' they seek to protect) and the state stands by and allows them to do so out of fear that to intervene would open them to the charge of racism. As I've noted elsewhere, '"culture" and "honour" here are, of course, the operative racialising terms, signalling an incorrigible Otherness defined by atavistic and insular gender roles and a violent, excessive masculinity that is, in the end, an over-compensation for an inherent lack of genuine manliness[29] – for the kind of respectable, bourgeois, civilised masculinity described in chapter 3. The 'grooming gangs' belong to sexual modernity's violent shadows and operate according to an unknown logic, moving in and out of our field of vision. The figure of the groomer thus provides an alibi for the organised abandonment of whole towns, for the neglect and denigration that made so many girls vulnerable to sexual exploitation.

The homegrown bomber, the Asian gang, and the Muslim child groomer complicate but do not entirely displace the idea of Asian men as 'thrifty, insular, academic and occasionally exotic'.[30] This figure – 'Other' but broadly unthreatening – is most easily trans-formed into a success story, into the 'model minority' who is an asset to multicultural Britain. It is this figure whom the novels and memoirs hope to vanquish through their stories of success, not as accountants or doctors but as journalists and graphic designers. Formed through the pressures of traditional family structures, hard work, academic success, and (crucially) sexual repression, this figure forms the back-drop for narratives of assimilation. This character is the least threatening, yet still characterised by a fundamental Otherness; he is drawn from the same waters as the babu. The model minority is dependent on the same conception of culture as the one from which the Asian gang and the homegrown terrorist emerge. Alexander observes, 'written into this attribution of cultural homogeneity and particularity are the seeds of its inevitable atrophy, a sense of cultural displacement and anachronism'.[31] As Muslim masculinity becomes the archetype for dangerous and threatening masculinity, this 'model minority' figure has been recoded as non-Muslim, as likely Hindu or Sikh.

## Surveillance, Incarceration, and Expulsion

*I'd say, if you hate this country so much, why don't you just fuck off to somewhere that's Muslim enough for you.*

Sarfraz Manzoor, Greetings from Bury Park

The mythologies and folk devils that animate Britain's racial regime are not only significant for their role in upholding a set of prejudices; they are crucial to the operation of racism itself. Islamophobia, as Kundnani observes, 'is more than a legitimizing shell that provides justification for state practices; it also causes them, as state surveillance agencies conjure into existence the very racial spectres they believe are haunting them, in a constant feedback loop of unintended consequences'.[32] The notion that Muslims spurn sexual modernity due to a set of uniquely backwards cultural proclivities is threaded through the War on Terror's transformations of 'the terms of civilian life'.[33] Regimes of surveillance, incarceration, indefinite detention, extradition, and torture depend on the view that Muslim 'terrorists' are not mere criminals (who could be subjected to criminal law), but are an epoch-defining threat to what is described, in the sentimental timbre of political rhetoric, as 'our way of life'.

The ideas I have discussed in this chapter are not merely latent in popular culture but manifest in political rhetoric and practice. In 2011, Prime Minister David Cameron spoke at the Security Conference at Munich, setting out a programme – referred to as 'muscular liberalism' – for responding to terrorism in Europe and beyond. In the speech, he asserts that 'the biggest threat that we face comes from terrorist attacks, some of which are, sadly, carried out by our own citizens'. Why do British citizens, young men born and bred in Britain, wish to kill their fellow citizens? Cameron's answer to the question comes in two parts: 'I believe the root lies in the existence of this extremist ideology. I would argue an important reason so many young Muslims are drawn to it comes down to a question of identity'. In this conception, the mere existence of extremist ideology loads the gun, but it is identity that pulls the trigger.

He suggests that a crisis in identity is the enabling or catalysing factor: 'In the UK, some young men find it hard to identify with the traditional Islam practiced at home by their parents, whose customs can seem staid when transplanted to modern Western countries. But these young men also find it hard to identify with Britain too, because we have allowed the weakening of our collective identity'.[34] The potential terrorist here is a victim of cultural excess, of a premodern clannishness out of step with the modern world. What right-wing ideologue Samuel Huntington termed the 'clash of civilizations', the ideological underpinnings of the War on Terror, is understood to play out within individuals – with dangerous consequences. In muscular liberalism, the firm hand of nationalism, shorn of outdated liberal niceties, is the only way to ensure that the identity crisis can be resolved in the direction of assimilation rather than violence.

As such, the notion of an identity crisis – an apparently benign trope – is used to justify and extend Britain's extensive counterter-rorism architecture. This architecture is embedded into everyday life in Britain and exported around the globe. The country's Prevent strategy – one of its central pillars – offers a particularly acute exam-ple of the way in which political rhetoric is intertwined with practices of policing, surveillance, incarceration, and deportation. As Azfar Shafi and Asim Qureshi observe, 'CVE [Countering Violent Extrem-ism] policies have begun to harmonise in line with the framework refined by Britain's Prevent and [be] promoted through multilateral forums such as the UN'.[35] Prevent began after the terrorist attacks in 2001, under New Labour, as an anti-radicalisation programme to fund the kinds of projects that the Cantle report recommended in order to merge the 'parallel lives' apparently lived by young Muslims in relation to white Britons. There was no obvious connection between funding five-a-side football and trips to Alton Towers and the attacks in the US, nor any evidence that these programmes were useful in preventing 'radicalisation', but Prevent continued to grow. After the

7/7 attacks in London, it developed into a network of surveillance embedded in Muslim communities, with 'community leaders' recruited into its structures. In 2015, the UK government pushed through the Counter-Terrorism and Security Act, a pernicious and far-reaching piece of legislation that mandated public-sector workers, including educators, social workers, and healthcare workers 'to have due regard to the need to prevent people from being drawn into terrorism'. The incorporation of unelected community leaders, the use of arts and leisure activities, and the embedding of surveillance into the structures of everyday life established the whole Muslim community as under suspicion and in need of reform.

The Prevent policy, particularly in the way it has become embedded in civil society, is best understood as an extension of colonial counterinsurgency, an approach to warfare that takes entire communities rather than individual actors as the enemy. As Rizwaan Sabir notes, 'It was in colonial India around the mid 1800s that the UK first began using methods of repression and social control against indigenous communities fighting to liberate their homeland from imperialism and colonialism by using low-level "hit and run" military tactics'.[36] While the methods of repression were diverse, they all operated on the basis of constructed racial knowledge. As Dirks observes, 'the ethnographic state was driven by the belief that India could be ruled using anthropological knowledge to understand and control its subjects and to represent and legitimate its own mission'.[37] In addition to more elaborate constructions, such as ascribing inherent criminality to particular groups, this 'knowledge' sometimes amounted to little more than the assertion of a crude racial hierarchy. The introduction of the 'dum-dum' bullet in 1896, for example, which exploded on impact rather than travelling cleanly through the body, was a brutal innovation based on the notion of an enemy closer to beast than man. As Wagner observes, given that British colonial officers were avid hunters, 'the most obvious source of inspiration was the types of ammunition used to shoot dangerous game such as tigers and rhinos'. The 'dum-dum' bullet was never used against a European enemy, with whom warfare was understood as a symmetrical process. Here, once again, we can see the rule of colonial difference by which the liberal promise through which colonial rule was justified can be suspended in the peripheries.

This suspension of liberal juridical norms, inherent to empire, has taken on a new life under the auspices of the War on Terror. The criminalisation of Muslim communities – whether through Prevent or more established forms of policing, such as stop-and-search – goes beyond racialised policing; rather, the 'War on Terror' has instated new forms of control, incarceration, banishment, and torture. The sexualised torture at Abu Ghraib offers a particularly disturbing example of the way in which the notion of Muslims as deviant outcasts from sexual modernity is deployed to justify brutal violence and degradation. Just as in the colonial 'ethnographic state', putatively anthropological insights regarding the 'Arab mind' are mobilised in the development of sexual violence as a practice of torture. As Deanna Heath observes, 'the sexual violation of colonized men and women was a means, therefore, of making them into obedient colonial subjects'.[38] In her writing on Abu Ghraib, Judith Butler notes that 'the torture was not merely an effort to find ways to shame and humiliate the prisoners of Abu Ghraib and Guantanamo on the basis of their presumptive cultural formation. The torture was also a way to coercively produce the Arab subject and the Arab mind'.[39] Torture was, Butler posits, 'a technique of modernization', used to demonstrate the superiority of Western sexual mores through the sexual humiliation of racial Others.[40] As such, we should consider sexual torture as a constitutive element of sexual modernity rather than as an aberration.

Further, even when sexuality is not explicitly present, the notion of Muslim masculinity as uniquely dangerous does significant work to undermine international norms around human rights. For example, Talha Ahsan, a young Muslim man from South London – a student of Arabic and a poet – was imprisoned for over six years without charge and then extradited to Florence supermax prison in the US on the basis of an alleged association with an Islamic news media website and publishing house from 1997 to 2004. In a medico-legal report of June 2009, a consultant psychiatrist described him as 'an extremely vulnerable individual who from a psychiatric perspective would be more appropriately placed in a specialist service for adults with autistic disorders'.[41] The charges were tenuous and there was no reason that he needed to be brought to the US. This flouting of human rights was only made possible by the rule of colonial difference that classifies Muslim men as uniquely dangerous rather than equally affected by the same types of ordinary neurodivergence that affect the rest of the population.

This reshaping of the norms of citizenship, national identity, and due process has been dramatically extended in recent years to go far beyond the remit of preventing terrorism. Abdul Aziz, Adil Khan, and Qari Abdul Rauf, who were convicted of offences that included rape, trafficking for sexual exploitation, and conspiracy to engage in sexual activity with a child alongside six others in Rochdale, have been stripped of their citizenship and are due to be deported to Pakistan at the end of their prison terms. Given the low levels of sexual abuse convictions, not to mention the well-documented state neglect of the victims of 'grooming gangs', the conviction of the perpetrators of these crimes is the exception, not the rule. Their deportation must be understood through the prism of race. It is only in the context of the War on Terror – and the racial regime it has calcified in contemporary Britain – that their banishment can be understood. In other words, though they were not convicted as 'terrorists', the bleak alchemy of race made their sexual crimes a matter of national security.

# 7

## Dangerous Brown Women

### Bodyguard

*Everywhere we are told that metropolitan liberals and their allegedly woke vanguard have embarked upon a righteous lifestyle project, one that effects an aggressive humiliation of the modest provincial majority.*

Sivamohan Valluvan

*Bodyguard*, which aired on BBC1 in 2018, opens with a gripping twenty-one-minute sequence.[1] Police sergeant David Budd is on a train with his two young children. Played by Richard Madden, David is handsome, square-jawed, blue-eyed, boyish still in his looks, but the picture of fatherly love in the care and attention he pays to his son and daughter. Through the window, he sees a tense exchange on the train platform – a conversation between a young South Asian woman in a black hijab and her presumed husband. A certain alertness shows immediately in his face. Soon after, it becomes clear that something is amiss. Viewers then see the woman he had observed from the window in the toilet of the train, strapped into a suicide vest and quivering in fear. As the toilet door opens and he sees the threat she poses – to himself and the other passengers, including his children – he greets her in Arabic with 'As-Salaam-Alaikum', the Islamic greeting meaning 'Peace be unto you'.

The bomb disposal unit, snipers, and counterterrorism forces are all quick to the scene. As the train is evacuated, the would-be bomber, Nadia, is in a bind: she doesn't want to detonate the bomb, but she is too scared to give herself up. By building a connection with Nadia

based first on his greeting and then on their shared vulnerability
('I'm scared too', he confirms) David coaxes Nadia out of the toilet
and into his arms. The embrace is ostensibly David's attempt to
protect her from the police sniper; as he informs her, he doesn't think
they'll shoot one of their own. But the image – a handsome white
man embracing a young Asian woman in a black hijab – signals more
than a plot point, indexing the West's longstanding fascination with
Muslim women's sexuality. David takes on the role of Nadia's protector and, as the series progresses, he is called upon by the police to
build on his rapport with her in order to extract intelligence.
Throughout, she appears meek, scared, childlike, still too scared of
her husband to divulge the information the police require. She claims
her husband used to lock her in the house, that she knew little of his
comings-and-goings, that he forced her to wear the suicide vest
against her will. In the final few minutes of the programme, in
Scooby-Doo–style exposition, it is revealed that Nadia is, in fact, the
bomb-maker. With a smirk, she observes that they were all so
convinced she was an 'oppressed Muslim woman' that they failed to
see that she was, in fact, an engineer who collaborated with organised
crime networks for 'guns and money' to promote 'Jihad'.

The initial portrayal of Nadia is also the making of David. It is
quickly revealed that David served in Afghanistan and has returned
home with the scars, physical and mental, of his suffering there. The
war in Afghanistan failed to neutralise the threat of 'Islamist terrorism', as the continued attacks depicted in the show attest. Instead, as
a veteran in the show observes, it simply brought aspects of war back
to London's streets. David is suffering from untreated PTSD, which
wrought havoc on his marriage (he is separated from his wife, Vicky,
a nurse). The hawkish home secretary, whom he is charged with
protecting and with whom he later has an affair, is at least partially
responsible for these prolonged wars. As noted, the war in Afghanistan was justified on the basis of the Taliban's oppressive, 'medieval'
misogyny. David's compassion – his cultural sensitivity, his confession
of his vulnerabilities, his desire to help Nadia – stands in for the
'good intentions' behind Western imperialism. The desire to help
oppressed Muslim women, the show suggests, is easily manipulated:

rather than helping meek, submissive victims of misogyny, is the West simply being duped by dangerous brown women?[2]

The world of the show is one in which the vast majority of those in positions of power are women or people of colour. The white men with institutional or political power are bit players with little screen time; in the world David inhabits, he is a minority. While it is common for television to depict the faces of power as more diverse than they are in reality (just think of Hollywood's Black police chiefs, judges, and high school principals), in *Bodyguard* this diversity serves a more precise purpose than progressive window dressing. Rather, this diversity freights David's vulnerability with gendered and racialised significance. This is a world of Islamist terrorists, bent coppers, scheming politicians, vengeful veterans, and violent gangsters. Corruption is rife. David stands alone at the mercy of nefarious powers. He is a sympathetic figure not in his honesty (which sometimes falters, though only when deceit is necessary) but in the simplicity of his desires: he wants only to be a husband and father. He wants only for the old promise of sexual modernity to be fulfilled. He has, after all, served Queen and country. By casting the figures of corruption and self-interest largely as women and racialised people, David's abiding heroism and innocence become confirmed as the unappreciated, even oppressed, properties of white masculinity. The image of a vulnerable white man as the victim of establishment corruption overseen by women and racial minorities is, of course, instrumental to the Brexit project and the nationalist convulsions that continue in its name.

*Bodyguard* also stages a shift from the Asian wife (of any religious background) as victim, in need of saving by state intervention, to the Muslim woman as violent 'Jihadi', a threat to the patriarchal order of the nation. Crucially, this shift depends on the premise that the image of the racialised woman as passive victim is part of a liberal conspiracy that enables racial Others to evade the state's grasp. Said observed that though Orientalism is notionally a discourse – a complex set of statements and practices – *about* the East, it tells us far more about the West's self-conception. Its portrayal of an imagined East reveals the anxieties, desires, and contradictions of the West from which the discourse travels, not the East it claims simply to document. One way to make use of this insight is to consider the ways in which the portrayal of racialised women is part of the making of white masculinity.

Turning to Gayatri Spivak's iconic formulation that 'white men are saving brown women from brown men',[3] we can discern that this triumvirate is co-constituting – the assumed patriarchy of the brown man necessitating the heroism of white men; the assumed heroism of white men the only source of help available to vulnerable brown women; the assumed vulnerability of brown women produced by the patriarchy of brown men – in an endless self-confirming loop. If the image of the vulnerable brown woman legitimises Western occupation, what does the image of the 'Jihadi bride' do? What kinds of state power are deployed against this new defector from sexual modernity? And does it matter in whose hands that power is concentrated?

## Inducting Muslim Women into Sexual Modernity

*In my experience as a professional woman and a mother, and somebody who has been on the margins of the political world, I have seen how all communities work more smoothly and productively when women are involved.*

Cherie Blair

In the early years of the War on Terror, though it was assumed Muslim women were unlikely to be 'radicalised', they were consistently the target of government interest, scrutiny, and policy interventions. While Muslim men were treated as potential terrorists, it was assumed that Muslim women held the keys to the problem of terrorism. Muslim women were treated like the 'black boxes' on the planes that were hijacked on 11 September 2001 – if only the West could get inside these mysterious objects, it would be possible to understand what had driven these strange bearded men to commit such opaque acts of violence. If this could be understood, they could be prevented from striking again.

The assumption that women offer a set of unique insights into a culture neither applies only to Muslim women, nor is it an innovation of the War on Terror. Mothers are assumed to take on the role of transmitting culture – of inducting children into traditions, particularly as they pertain to clothing, food, and other visible markers of cultural specificity. As women are assumed to be responsible for cultural knowledge, they are targeted as conduits for cultural transformation. And as we have seen, the notion of culture is sutured to sexuality. Further, in the Western philosophical tradition, women are viewed as a source of spiritual authority whose influence on the public sphere should be made indirectly, through their husbands. According to John Ruskin, for example, a woman's role is to watch over, teach and guide men – acting as a counsellor but not a political actor in her own right.[4] It is this view of gender complementarity and the role of women that was reheated in the early years of the War on Terror, in the assumption that Muslim women could exert a restraining influence on their husbands, sons, and brothers.

Of course, the notion that Muslim women might be able to restrain the violent impulses of 'their' men was complemented by the narrative of Muslim women's unique oppression – a trope so ubiquitous that it could be referenced explicitly on prime-time television in *Bodyguard*. Muslim women's oppression was precisely the rationale used to justify the invasion and occupation of Afghanistan as a moral rather than merely strategic endeavour. Across the political divide, commentators and politicians lined up to confirm that the West was going to 'save' Muslim women from the unique patriarchal violence of the Taliban. The distinctive aesthetics of the Taliban – the images of women in blue burqas against the backdrop of desert and rubble – were particularly germane for the Western political imaginary, not least because the role of the US in producing both the Taliban and the rubble were consistently obscured. Instead, the images circulated as evidence of a relentless Oriental backwardness. The footage of women unveiling and crowds celebrating in the immediate aftermath of the Taliban's initial defeat at the hands of American and British troops seemed to confirm that white men with guns and tanks really could liberate brown women.

Back in Britain, this notion that Muslim women needed saving was also operationalised. The old archetype of the oppressed Asian woman provided some animating force, but the category of Muslim also offered a new logic that both built on and transformed older racial regimes. Muslim women were not only South Asian but could trace their roots to every continent. Naaz Rashid's research into the UK's domestic counterterrorism strategy in the early 2000s shows the ways in which women were targeted for 'empowerment'. As Rashid puts it, 'The association between empowerment and Muslim women has a common sense appeal because of two factors: the perceived status of women in Islam and secondly, given that the majority of Muslims in the UK are of South Asian origin, (post) colonial constructions of the "submissive Asian woman"'.[5] It was assumed that, if Muslim women were to take up the promise of sexual modernity – if they were to enter the labour market and self-realise as individuals – then they could prevent their husbands, brothers, or sons from committing acts of terror.

A particularly revealing programme described by Rashid is the 'role models roadshow' which aimed to 'raise aspirations' by sending Muslim women successful in particular careers to speak to young Muslim women and girls across the country. In his work on policing, Elliott-Cooper identifies mentoring and role model programmes in black communities, deployed by liberal and conservative elements alike, as interventions which depend on the notion that racialised families are dysfunctional and damaging. He suggests that these programmes obscure the operation of racism and deflect responsibility onto apparently defective black family structures. As he puts it, 'these programmes explain away racial inequality through a character deficit within each member of the Black family'.[6] A similar logic is at play in the programmes funded through Prevent, in which state intervention is supposed to compensate for the lack of opportunity and ambition produced by downtrodden mothers, overbearing fathers, and daughters trapped between two cultures. These programmes, then, are not only to function as career training, but as spaces of pedagogy in which young women learn that only individualism, brokered by the nation-state, can guarantee happiness, freedom, and opportunity.

Rashid reads these programmes in line with the ways that women in the Global South are targeted for 'development'.[7] As Kalpana Wilson explains, women are seen as more 'efficient' neoliberal subjects, whose education, controlled fertility, and entry into the workplace will act as a counterbalance to the assumed corruption or fecklessness of indigenous patriarchies.[8] It is commonly accepted that young women hold the key to ending world poverty: healthy and well-educated girls are expected to marry later and have fewer children. Through their improved economic prospects, it is hoped that the fate of the Global South will be transformed. Of course, missing from this account are the brutal forces of global inequality: structural adjustment programmes, debt, war and militarisation, and the effects of accelerating ecological breakdown. Nonetheless, this logic is 'brought home' to Britain and applied to Muslim women. The overall effect of targeting Muslim women for 'empowerment' is not only to strengthen the neoliberal incarnation of sexual modernity, but to fortify the category of 'Muslim woman'. As local authorities were encouraged to fund projects that 'empower Muslim women', organisations in need of financial support began to emphasise their 'Muslimness', even if the issues they were addressing transcended religion. This dynamic became further entrenched as austerity began to bite after 2010.

Alongside the mentoring programmes, theology seminars, and sports projects, more subtle, insidious tactics have been deployed in an attempt to reshape Muslim women's subjectivity. For example, the platform SuperSisters was launched in 2015. Aimed at Muslim girls and young women, it described itself as 'a global platform for young Muslimahs in east London to share and create inspiring and empowering content'; it included content about faith, self-care, television, new year's resolutions, and travel all presented in millennial pink. In the same year, a digital platform, This Is Woke, was launched by J-Go Media, a company describing itself as 'a not-for-profit community group' that has two decades of experience of engaging with Muslim communities in East London. Content included uplifting videos ('Meet the Syrian ballet dancer using art to defy terror'), motivational graphics ('Take a self-care break' on a mint green background), and inspiring quotations ('When people are determined, they can overcome anything' over a picture of Nelson Mandela).

It emerged, however, that these platforms were funded by the Research, Information and Communications Unit (RICU), a strategic communications unit within the Office for Security and Counter-Terrorism. These websites were not made *by* young Muslim women, but *for* young Muslim women, aiming to reshape their subjectivity in line with the promise of sexual modernity. Yahya Birt describes this process as astroturfing, 'designed to give the appearance of "grass roots" mobilisation or community-led bottom-up civil society initiatives, when in fact it is driven from above by state funding, patronage, training, in-kind services, etc. channelled through proxies'.[9] This approach draws from the handbook of counterinsurgency, treating entire communities as under suspicion. To understand why these covert information campaigns were developed in 2015, we need to consider the figure of the 'jihadi bride' against whom they were constructed.

## Jihadi Brides

*Unmasked, the ISIS bride of Twickenham: How a mother-of-three, 31, raised in an affluent West London suburb is now languishing in the same Syrian refugee camp as Shamima Begum.*

                                                              Daily Mail

As Islamic State began to take territory in Syria and Iraq in 2014, it quickly become clear that they had global reach and were making careful use of social media and encrypted messaging apps. Alongside images of beheadings and reports of mass rape, stories circulated of young people from Western countries covertly travelling across the globe to join the caliphate. While men formed the first wave of global recruits, they were quickly joined by young women. That Islamic State's women recruits were often intelligent and well-educated (and included white converts) only added to the sense of confusion and horror. By 2015, it was estimated that Western women made up over

550, or 10 per cent, of IS's Western foreign fighters. In the British media, the women that Islamic State recruits have been the source of endless fascination. Though a global phenomenon, so many Britons travelled to join IS that Manbji, a town close to the Turkish border in northern Syria, was dubbed 'Little London'. After the decades of political rhetoric about 'saving Muslim women', the 'Jihadi bride' was met with a deep sense of both rage and anxiety. This anxiety is evoked by the nomenclature of 'Jihadi bride' itself. Translated as struggling or striving, 'jihad' is a term used to refer to all kinds of spiritual effort but circulates in the West as the signifier of 'Islamist terror'. The conjunction of a word that conjures epochal violence with the highly gendered and somewhat anachronistic implications of 'bride' offers a particularly potent tabloid spin on the phenomenon of Western IS recruits, suggesting a uniquely rogue racialised femininity.

This sense of the IS recruit as the embodiment of subversive sexuality has been particularly powerful in the context of the widespread view of Muslim women as eternal victims. As Lila Abu-Lughod observes, 'when you save someone, you imply that you are saving her from something. You are also saving her to something'.[10] The implicit question that underpinned the salacious news coverage and social media commentary was this: Why did Muslim women not want what they were being saved to? Why did the consumerism, careerism, and restaurant reviews in millennial pink on the SuperSisters website not do the trick? Why did they fail to be 'empowered' by the role models roadshow? Why would they turn away from the promise of sexual modernity?

To understand the obsession with the figure of the Jihadi bride, we need to return to the Orientalist construction of Muslim women. In the Orientalist imaginary, the Muslim woman is a phantasm organised around the veil and the harem, both visual tropes that condense deception, opacity, containment, and resistance to exposure. There is a significant body of work on these tropes in Algeria which, though a French colony, has played a crucial role in the wider European construction of the licentious East, and thus continues to animate the racial regime of contemporary Britain. As Frantz Fanon identified in his analysis of the Algerian anticolonial struggle, the

French had 'a precise political doctrine': 'If we want to destroy the structure of Algerian society, its capacity for resistance, we must first of all conquer the women'.[11] This is, of course, precisely the same logic that underpins the Prevent programme's interventions into Muslim women's lives.

The notion of women's foundational social power became centred on Algerian women's dress, specifically the practice of veiling. In Meyda Yeğenoğlu's extension of Fanon's argument, she explains, 'With the help of this opaque veil, the Oriental woman is considered as not yielding herself to the Western gaze and therefore imagined as hiding something behind the veil. It is through the inscription of the veil as a mask that the Oriental woman is turned into an enigma'.[12] Unveiling Muslim women – as French troops did in Algeria – was a violation, therefore, not only of women's bodily autonomy and religious belief, but of a perceived unwillingness to yield to the Western gaze. The opacity of the veil was a unique affront precisely because, as Yeğenoğlu puts it, 'With modernity comes a new form of institutional power which is based on visibility and transparency and which refuses to tolerate areas of darkness'.[13] Darkness, as symbolised by the veil, was viewed as the breeding ground for anticolonial opposition.

In the Algerian independence struggle, women began to see the veil within the terms in which the coloniser had portrayed it, albeit refracted through a political commitment to national liberation: 'The affirmation of the veil in the anti-colonial struggle was a direct response to the colonial desire to unveil, reveal, and control the colonised country. It is not surprising after all that women's agency emerged out of the texture of their own culture'.[14] The veil became, therefore, a symbol of their agency. Religious dress was also a highly effective means of concealing weapons, thus producing as reality precisely the threatening Oriental woman that the West has invented as phantasm. As Mary Ann Doane asserts, anticolonial women guerrillas enacted a 'defamiliarised version' of this phantasm.[15]

I suggest that in the most infamous and overdetermined example of the 'Jihadi bride', Shamima Begum, we might see a similar dynamic at play. This is not to suggest that Begum is a figure of anticolonial liberation. Rather, I want to show the ways in which the ascription of racial status is profoundly unstable; the tropes used to determine one's status can be taken up and used to new, sometimes troubling, ends. Indeed, this process is crucial to both the maintenance and the overturning of racial regimes. Shamima Begum travelled to join IS with two of her school friends, Kadiza Sultana and Amira Abase. Sultana was killed in an air strike at age seventeen and Abase's whereabouts are unknown. Begum, however, has become a figure of constant speculation. At the time of writing, she is living in a refugee camp, after having her citizenship revoked by the British state. Begum has been the source of such fascination, partly due to the ways she has represented both her motivations for joining IS and her life within their jurisdiction. In an interview in 2019, in which she expressed her desire to return to Britain to raise her son, she said, 'When I went to Syria I was just a housewife for the entire four years. Stayed at home, took care of my kids'. I suggest that there is something notable in this defence: Muslim women have long been considered 'merely housewives' – in claiming this position in her defence, she becomes the uncanny double of the 'oppressed Muslim woman' who the British state claims to want to save.

Begum's claim to being 'just a housewife' has largely been ignored and instead her pleas for 'sympathy' have been read against the backdrop of her firm association with violence. She claims to have taken seeing her first severed head in stride, to have been unfazed by beheadings, and to have responded to the rape of Yazidi women by stating that 'Shia do the same in Iraq'. Begum's apparent lack of remorse has been the subject of much discussion, often invoked to justify making her stateless. Some left and feminist commentary observes that her flat delivery and apparent lack of emotion could be a trauma response. Though this intervention is useful, it may be less so in the long term than simply insisting that no one should be made stateless. Rather than offer a defence of Begum, it might be useful to think about what work the obsession with her as a political figure does for the nationalist project.

I want to suggest that there is something in her association with violence that explains the ways in which she remains a figure of disgust and fascination. More broadly, something is compelling about a woman engaged in or supportive of violence, all the more so when she is racialised. Begum's constant presence in the public eye helps to justify the suspension of ordinary juridical processes. The obsessive demonisation of Begum by the right-wing press is used to solidify the notion that the niceties of the liberal project have produced a soft, emasculated British nation which must re-establish itself around a more strident, conservative isolationism. If even the women who so badly need to enter sexual modernity don't want to, then why should we continue to indulge them? While the notion that Muslim women need 'saving' is used to justify military occupation abroad and militarised policing at home, the assumption that Muslim women pose a unique threat to Western democracy also comes with violent, racialising consequences, used to justify highly punitive modes of exclusion and to stoke a virulent, street-based racism. The message is clear: assimilate into sexual modernity or feel the full force of the law – there will be no exceptions made for victims of patriarchy.

## The Seductions of Sadism

*If you had the ultimate punishment for the murder of policemen and other heinous crimes, I am sure it would act as a deterrent. We must send a clear signal to people that crime doesn't pay. The punishment must fit the crime and yes, I do support capital punishment.*

Priti Patel, 2006

While the home secretary who stripped Shamima Begum of her British citizenship was Sajid Javid, he was quickly succeeded in this Cabinet role by Priti Patel, who has made it clear that Begum will not be allowed to return to British shores, even to appeal her loss of citizenship, even though making someone stateless contravenes international law. Patel is an interesting figure to contrast with Shamima Begum. In this section, I'll consider what work these two figures – racialised, gendered, and associated with violence – do in the national imaginary. Rather than attempt to investigate their psychology (about which I cannot claim any particular knowledge), I address the role

they perform in the development of an increasingly virulent, isolationist, and authoritarian nationalism. If we understand these two
figures as co-constituted in the national imaginary, taking shape
against each other, some interesting dynamics come to the surface.

I take my inspiration from Jacqueline Rose's essay on Margaret
Thatcher and Ruth Ellis, the last woman to be put to death for murder
in Britain. Rose asks, 'what happens when it is a woman who comes
to embody the social at its most perverse?'[16] In attempting to answer
this question through an examination of Patel and Begum, I suggest
that we might be able to see how the violence of Britain's racial regime
comes to be viewed as natural or inevitable. Further, as this violence
becomes embodied by racialised women, we can see the ways in
which, from the fractures in sexual modernity, new forms of racial
exclusion can be justified.

An older racial logic might view them both as 'British Asian', but,
as I've tried to show, this is a community divided vertically by class as
well as by religion, national origin, caste, and gender. In many ways,
these figures could not be further apart. After all, Shamima Begum
was groomed online as a teenager, has suffered the loss of three
children, and has been made stateless. She lives in a refugee camp in
Syria with little hope of seeing her family again. Patel has lived a life
of ease: she went to university, completed a master's degree, interned
at the Conservative Central Office before taking a job at the public
relations consultancy firm Weber Shandwick. There she worked on
the British American Tobacco account, for which she attempted to
manage their public image after it came to light that their Burma
factory was underpaying workers and funding the military dictator-
ship. After a brief fling with the Referendum Party, Patel returned
to the Conservatives and was quickly identified as a promising candidate by new party leader David Cameron. She has since taken up a
prominent role on the far right of the party.

Despite these differences, a crude liberal antiracism views them
both through the prism of identity. It is assumed that Patel's violent
policies are the result of 'internalised racism' – that she is, somehow,
overcompensating for the racial prejudice she has (apparently)
received and attempting to seek the favour of her erstwhile

oppressors. Begum's defection to Islamic State is also viewed through the lens of identity, through the 'culture clash' model described in chapter 6, now applied to young women rather than men. To reiterate, this view suggests that Begum, unable to manage the conflict between Western sexual freedoms and the more conservative values of her parents, has opted instead for the apparently nihilistic certainties of the caliphate. These interpretations belong to the same intellectual universe; they view political choices as psychologically determined, a view that derives from the individuations of sexual modernity. This approach offers a simple psychological fix, obscuring what may be most disturbing: that people use their agency in ways that are cruel, contradictory, violent, or unintelligible to us. Perhaps it is easier to believe that Patel is suffering from 'internalised racism' than that she is, herself, simply a racist. Perhaps it's easier to believe that Begum has been duped or tricked than that she believed in the political vision of Islamic State. In many ways, Begum encapsulates a thorny contradiction: though sexual modernity demands that we make use of our agency, it sanctions only very limited forms of self-realisation.

Patel describes herself as a Thatcherite and often rehearses the language of meritocracy and assimilation that was a cornerstone of Thatcher's political rhetoric. Patel is of Ugandan Asian extraction – a double diaspora community heavily courted by Thatcher as providing the model for assimilable immigrants. South Asians in East Africa played a comprador role in the economy of the British Empire, embracing their position as traders and merchants alongside their preferential treatment over the native people. As Neha Shah puts it, they were the 'subcolonial agents of civilisation', there to keep Africans 'in order'.[17] When Africanisation policies across East Africa were enacted in the 1960s and 1970s, many Kenyan and Ugandan Asians came to Britain, a significant number of whom were keen to present themselves as loyal British subjects, eager to pick up their business interests back in the mother country. Though East African Asians comprise a minority of the South Asians in Britain, their economic success has given them disproportionate political influence. Patel's rise to power must be viewed in light of this history.

But despite Patel seeing herself as a Thatcherite, her politics argu- ably lie to the right of Thatcher. As home secretary, she oversaw some of the most draconian legislation ever enacted in Britain, with a sharp focus on criminalising freedom of movement and political dissent. At the height of the coronavirus pandemic in 2020, for example, she insisted on housing people seeking asylum in derelict army barracks, despite public health advice that confirmed they would be unsafe. Then, the 2022 Nationality and Borders Act was introduced, effectively criminalising seeking asylum in the UK by making entry into the country without permission a criminal offence, carrying a sentence of up to four years' imprisonment. Perhaps the most prominent aspect of the Act is one that enables the Home Office to strip people of their citizenship without notice if it would 'not be reasonably practicable' in the interests of national security or of the 'relationship between the United Kingdom and another country'. The case of Shamima Begum is, of course, a key touchstone in the devel- opment of citizenship stripping as a mode of governance which produces a highly stratified racial regime.

While Thatcher presented herself as a maternal figure – a firm- but-fair mother to the nation, balancing the national economy as a wife and mother manages the household budget – Patel embodies a more subversive femininity. Here we can begin to see the ways in which the nuclear family no longer functions as the obvious or inevitable correlate to the individual. While political figures have historically demonstrated their familial qualities, emphasising their role *in loco parentis* to the population, the fracturing of sexual moder- nity has loosened this demand. The ascendancy of figures such as Donald Trump and Boris Johnson – whose aggressive sexual indis- cretion appears to be part of their appeal rather than making them unsuitable for office – evidences the shifting ground on which ques- tions of sex and political power are negotiated.

On this new terrain, Patel has been able to craft a more individ- uated, unencumbered persona. Indeed, it is this unrestrained quality that has become her hallmark. Her disregard for democratic process came to widespread public attention in 2017 after it was revealed that, as international development secretary, she had scheduled a series of unauthorised meetings with the government of Israel which breached the Ministerial Code. A series of bullying allegations made by civil servants who had worked with her confirmed this disregard for appropriate conduct or behaviour. This disregard is part of her appeal. As standards of living drop, many experience the world as capricious and arbitrary. Following the rules – by getting a job, by maintaining family life – offers little protection from sickness, ecological disaster, inconvenience, or suffering. Patel does not follow the rules – but she gets away with it. And just as importantly, she does so in the name of nationalism. As Rose notes, 'a law-breaker at the summit of politics is enticing'.[18] Through the spectacle of Patel's disdain for the rules, she offers a form of catharsis to a viewer aligned with the nation and its claims to superiority.

Patel's is not the coerced cruelty of the minor functionary – this is no 'banality of evil' – but the active, magnifying-glass-on-hot-stone violence of the sadist. Indeed, Patel regularly behaves with precisely the duplicitousness, disregard for the mores of liberal political culture, and maniacal devotion to cruelty that the West might expect from an Oriental despot. It is telling that the reboot of puppet show *Spitting Image* depicts her as a dominatrix, taking sadistic pleasure from enacting racist, sexist policies under the cover of being a brown woman. Given that the satirical bent of *Spitting Image* has been rather neutered – indeed, it is now accepted that Tory politicians relish their depiction on the show, that it functions less as critique than as tribute – it is fair to assume that this portrayal of Patel confirms rather than undermines the public persona she has crafted.

Rose's analysis of Thatcher and Ellis helps to illuminate what might be at stake here: 'Drawing attention to themselves precisely as women, they can serve to gloss over that double and paradoxical location of violence – the perversion of the state in relation to violence can be transposed on to the perversity of the woman, its more troubling implications then siphoned off and ignored'.[19] In this case, the most violent excesses of state power – making people stateless, criminalising protest, pursuing policies that directly lead to people drowning in the Channel – can become associated with Patel's sadistic personality. While it is common to assume her value to the Tories is to function as an alibi against the charge of racism, I suggest that instead she serves to further entrench the notion that racism is a left-wing conspiracy theory. In the process, the gratuitous and improvisatory ways in which the sovereign state uses its monopoly on violence are hidden from view.

If we view Patel and Begum together, not as equivalents but as key players in the fracturing and recomposing of sexual modernity, we can see the work race continues to do in justifying violence. Begum is the source of such disturbed fascination precisely because she articulates an uncomfortable truth: that the violence of Islamic State cannot be severed from the violence of 'ordinary' nation-states: assassination, organised sexual violence, and banishment are part of the War on Terror too. Further, she draws attention to the way in which, when women become national symbols, the disavowed labour of social reproduction becomes momentarily visible. She insists, perhaps inadvertently, on the central role of the ordinary housewife, the citizen who turns a blind eye, as essential to state violence. For this, it seems, she must be punished again and again. Here we can see the drama of liberalism's demise played out by brown women – they provide not progressive cover, but a kind of perverse pleasure. Their association with violence serves to shift the discourse away from the shibboleth that Asian women need saving by the West to one in which it is possible to state that no one needs saving, that no one is worth saving, that migrants should drown, and groomed teenage girls should be left stateless in refugee camps. This is a twist on biopolitics – not only who is made to live or allowed to die, but who violates, deports, kills, and who watches in rapt fascination, uncertain if this violence done in their name will be done to them next.

## Fractured Promises

*The old world is dying and the new cannot yet be born and in this interregnum a variety of morbid symptoms appear.*

Gramsci

As we've seen, the female Islamic State recruit – the 'Jihadi bride' – is such a disturbing figure partly because she dissents from sexual modernity. This dissent has an ironic character within Britain's racial regime – if Asian women, then Muslim women, have been seen as 'mere housewives', the seizure of this position in direct opposition to the British state has an uncanny force, though not, I am suggesting, a progressive one. The so-called 'Jihadi brides', however, are not the only dissenters or refuseniks from the promise of sexual modernity. Many other peculiar figures are arising. The fracturing of sexual modernity, the sense in which the search for a romantic partner may not be sufficient consolation for the deterioration of our living conditions, is producing some strange bedfellows.

Racial regimes crumble and recompose, and the mythologies through which they are maintained shift. As Chitty puts it, 'Against the background of widespread infrastructural fallout, the normal persists within decrepit forms, remaining in force but with significantly weakened powers'.[20] The social relations under which the nuclear family is a viable way to organise one's life no longer hold in Britain. As Gargi Bhattacharyya observes, 'waged work no longer enables workers to form relationships, create homes, care for loved ones, recuperate before recommencing work, and perhaps even raise children'. As economic conditions can no longer support nuclear family life, the old mythology of sexual modernity – its images, narratives, promises – is losing its lustre and new modes of sexual ethics, gendered subjectivity, and kinship are emerging. Dating and hook-up apps have inaugurated new practices of casual sex, and new grammars of gender expression are popularised on social media. Some developments in sexual politics – a militant transfeminism, alternative gender identities moving into the mainstream, the rise of polyamory – are a conscious attempt to embrace the liberatory possibilities of sexual modernity by severing its connections to the nuclear family. Others take the cruellest aspects of sexual modernity and organise a vicious, reactionary, or violent sexual politics from these fragments.

Digital life has propelled new subcultures organised around violent masculinity. While many of the central ideas around which these groups form have a long history, social media platforms, particularly YouTube and Reddit, have incubated new organisations, both informal and formal, to develop and disseminate these ideas. Men's rights activists (MRAs), involuntary celibates (incels), and QAnon supporters are three such groups whose influence has quickly come to be felt in the mainstream. Incels offer a particularly acute insight into contemporary life. Though the term was coined by a woman attempting to find solace among others who were struggling with the absence of romantic love or sexual connection, incels are now a distinctly masculine phenomenon: indeed, gendered hierarchy is at the heart of this subculture, as incels claim that it is not even possible for women to be involuntarily celibate. Incels believe the world is dominated by a strict sexual Darwinism, in which women aim to improve their evolutionary prospects by having sex with higher status men. In this schema – which bears more than a passing resemblance to Jordan Peterson's endorsement of sexual and gendered hierarchy, described in chapter 2 – women can easily 'trade up' (so a '7 out of 10' woman might 'bag herself' a '9 out of 10' man), leaving men at the lower ranks unable to access sex, care, romance, or companionship. These men do not dissent from sexual modernity; rather, they take its implicit sexual marketplace as the fundamental and relentless motor of civilisation. They do not object to its hierarchies; rather, they object to their place within this order.

These hierarchies are fundamentally racial in nature, organised around precisely the colonial schema that places whiteness at the apex of sexual civilisation. Incels want to sleep with 'hot blond sluts'; South and East Asian incels claim to be sexually marginalised on the basis of race but deride non-white women; black men are viewed as unfairly desired, as somehow 'gaming' the sexual marketplace. The multiracial nature of this subculture – even as it affirms a racial hierarchy – is suggestive of the shifts in racial mythology that co-constitute the fractures in sexual modernity. New racial myths are being made from the sediments of colonial sexual cultures, reanimated by patriarchal ressentiment incubating in digital life.

In its final episode, *Bodyguard*'s hero awakens, bloodied and groggy from a beating at the hands of the gang with whom the Islamist cell is conspiring, to find himself strapped into a suicide vest. It appears that, in a world in which the nation-state has been infiltrated by deceitful women and subversive racial Others, David has become the duped and innocent victim that Nadia posed as in the opening scene. Like Nadia, he is soon surrounded by armed officers – this time, though, he leads them through the deserted streets of London to his home, where he can produce the evidence of conspiracy that will clear his name. By embodying the manly virtues of courage and honour, he can restore his position – and implicitly heal the ailing national polity. After all its improbable twists and turns, *Bodyguard* circles round to a happy ending. David Budd finally accepts counselling for his PTSD; his wife Vicky takes him back; and the heterosexual family is restored. While always trite, in this instance, the ending rings especially hollow – a magical solution to a drama that has registered the disruptions to white masculinity but not the disruptions made in an attempt to conserve its power.

# 8

## Think of the Children

### No Outsiders

*In the original* No Outsiders *book I referenced radicalisation briefly; however since then I have been developing the resource with a specific aim to prevent young people from being drawn in to terrorism, rather than as a resource simply to promote equality and diversity*

Andrew Moffat

In January 2019, parents of children at Parkfield Community School in Saltley, Birmingham, launched a petition against the 'No Outsiders' curriculum which was being taught at the primary level. Dissent soon spread to other schools in Birmingham, including Anderton Park Primary School in Balsall Heath, where parents began to protest the No Outsiders programme outside the school gates. In May 2019, the High Court banned the protests outside Anderton Park, imposing an exclusion zone around the school. The curriculum itself was part of 'Relationships and Sex Education' (RSE) for primary schools, piloted at the school in 2014 by assistant head teacher Andrew Moffat.

The No Outsiders curriculum developed out of an Economic and Social Research Council-funded research project on approaches to 'sexualities inequality' in primary schools which ran between 2006 and 2008 across sixteen primary schools in England. Moffat was one of the researcher-practitioners involved and, following the end of that project, developed the No Outsiders curriculum which became a recognisable brand in 2019, the name at the heart of another of the racially charged moral panics around sex that remain a constant feature of life in Britain. The curriculum, as the protestors noted, was part of the school's fulfilment of the Prevent duty – a presentation to the government depicted the project as an essential part of the school's duty to teach 'Fundamental British Values' in a bid to 'reduce radicalisation'. Unsurprisingly, parents objected to the notion that their children were 'at risk' of being 'radicalised' and that LGBT RSE would inoculate them against this hazard.

This national spectacle coalesced around questions of gender as well as sexual orientation. While 'transgender' has long been included in the acronym LGBT, trans people have largely been marginalised within rights struggles, particularly as these movements have been institutionalised through political parties and NGOs. As such, it was notable (and relatively novel), that trans people played a prominent part in the No Outsiders curriculum, with a children's book called *Julian is a Mermaid* by Jessica Love, which depicted a trans character, attracting significant attention in media coverage of the protests. While the meteoric rise of gay rights chipped away at the system of complementary gender roles as the basis for romantic love, the gender dyad itself largely remained intact into the early years of the twenty-first century. More recently, however, trans politics has gained significant ground. Sexual modernity's promise of self-realisation has now been taken up in a new register, with gender expression increasingly understood as an essential dimension of one's autonomy. There is growing acceptance and embrace of non-binary identities. While some argue this instates a 'gender trinary' in the place of a binary, the sense of widespread dissidence from the strictures of the dyad has proven politically significant. Despite the limitations of this ascendant gender system, there is ample evidence that the old certainties of sex and gender – of the sexed body and its attendant social roles – are breaking down. Indeed, the inclusion of trans issues in the LGBT RSE curriculum is evidence of a significant shift.

The growing scepticism about the naturalness of the sexed body and its inevitable production of gendered social roles has not, however, gone uncontested. There has been significant reactionary pushback. In the UK – as in Brazil, Italy, Poland, and elsewhere – organised transphobia has become a significant node in a wider ecology of an ascendant – if inchoate – fascism. Transphobia, however, has not only come from traditional conservative elements but has been articulated by a small section of right-wing feminists who travel under the sign of 'radical feminism'. As Sophie Lewis points out, 'In both frameworks, sexuate difference is naturalised and seen as preceding class. Whereas conservative Christians like to make class invisible and underline the sacred naturalness of procreative purpose, radfems by and large theorise a binarising interpretation of reproductive biology as class'.[1] This disturbing alliance – between conservative Christians and reactionary feminists – is symptomatic of a new political modality exemplified by the No Outsiders conflict, in which unexpected alliances are temporarily brokered through moral panics or conspiracy theories.

To understand why this relatively contained conflict took on such mainstream significance, we must look to the visual spectacle of the protests. In the images of women in hijab and men with beards holding placards reading 'Adam and Eve, not Adam and Steve', several salacious tropes came together. The 'culture clash' described in the previous chapters seemed to be perfectly encapsulated by the images of religious devotion and racialised anger. Further, as Pride has been transformed from queer protest to family-friendly corporate parade, homophobic demonstrations are received as an anachronism. In particular, the biblical register of this placard seemed to recall the God Hates Fags protests organised by the Westboro Baptist Church of Topeka in the US, which became iconic symbols of cultish religious homophobia across the Western world in the 1990s and early 2000s. The glut of news coverage about the protests in Birmingham generated a tremendous volume of interviews and op-eds, hashtags, and Instagram graphics. Debates on LGBT RSE became a mainstay of daytime TV and talk radio.

The spectacle was particularly potent coming as it did at the end of a long decade of Tory-led government in which homonationalist rhetoric had become a familiar touchstone. Under the coalition government, gay rights were explicitly linked to an imperialist agenda. In 2011, Cameron pledged to cut aid to African nations where homosexuality remained illegal, regardless of the fact that these laws have their origins in British colonial legislation. As Rao notes, this announcement sparked hostile responses from political leaders in Tanzania, Ghana, and Uganda, as well as from African LGBT activists who warned that 'gay conditionality' could put them at risk of further scapegoating and violence.[2]

Cameron rearticulated this logic in a new, more upbeat form a couple of years later: in an attempt to make further political capital out of gay marriage, he suggested it could be an export good. He said, 'Many other countries are going to want to copy this. And, as you know, I talk about the global race, about how we've got to export more and sell more so I'm going to export the bill team. I think they can be part of this global race and take it around the world'. By articulating his aim in the language of global capitalism, precisely in terms of 'the global race', of the imperative to 'export more and sell more', Cameron was able to cleave together international markets and gay marriage, with Britain as a leading player across the cultural, political, social, and economic spheres. Further, as Rao notes, 'Conservative support for same-sex marriage timed perfectly with the drive to reprivatise social welfare through family promotion in a time of austerity'.[3] Gay families become 'folded into life', to use Puar's term[4] – a metonym for the national family – while homophobes become the enemy within.

In this chapter, I'll consider the No Outsiders controversy over sex education as heralding a political shift. Sexual modernity is still used to racialise Muslim communities, but the fractures in sexual modernity are also creating a space for new and unpredictable alliances to take hold. This is a key moment of convergence, in which we can see multiple nationalisms competing for dominance. The Islamophobic homonationalism of the early years of the War on Terror must now contend with other nationalisms of a different provenance and flavour, articulated through reactionary gender politics and attempts to conserve the sexual dyad. We'll see how global networked nationalisms make strategic alliances on the basis of transphobia with precisely the racialised communities British nationalism seeks to expel in other moments. These unexpected convergences confound liberal sensibilities and create new opportunities for ethnonationalist recruitment. The figure of the child is mobilised in these ruptures to sexual modernity, and in the new racial regimes recomposing in the surge of global nationalisms.

## The Child

*We can't simply be telling children that their beliefs are wrong or unaccept-able; we have to be delivering a curriculum that enables children to understand the benefits that exist in a society where diversity and differences are celebrated. Furthermore we need our children to want to be part of that society, and we have to sell it to them; that desire may not come naturally by itself.*

Andrew Moffat

Across the political spectrum, the No Outsiders controversy was viewed through the figure of the child. Each actor framed their intervention as one made in defence of children – whether their own, those of the community or nation, or their own child self. As Jenny Kitzinger observes, childhood is 'an institution and ideal which exists independently from, and sometimes in spite of, actual flesh and blood children'.[5] Arguably, even when children are not the explicit subject of a political crisis, their presence is always implied: as Lee Edelman puts it '[the] figural Child alone embodies the citizen as an ideal, entitled to claim full rights to its future share in the nation's good . . . the fantasy subtending the image of the Child invariably shapes the logic within which the political itself must be thought'.[6] As the representation of the future, the child remains the condition of the political itself.

Crucially, however, childhood is not an essential condition, the same across all times and places, but a social classification that has been historically constituted. The notion of children as ontologically distinct from – and in need of protection by – adults began to circu-late at the advent of modernity. As such, the child plays a crucial role in sexual modernity, as the figure whose sexuality is both most pre-cious and most perverse. In Foucault's genealogy of sexuality, he identifies schools and the family as the sites where the regulation of children's sexuality is at its most severe and productive. Masturbation is the subject of constant worry, necessitating surveillance within both the educational context and the home. The preoccupation with child sexuality was not evenly distributed; it was stratified by race and class. As Kitzinger insists, the image of a white, bourgeois child is used to represent childhood itself – that is, a state of essential innocence.[7] Working-class children in the imperial centre and children in the colonies were viewed as already possessing something akin to adult sexuality, while the sexuality of children within the bourgeois family generated intense anxiety. As Carolyn Steedman observes, working-class children understood themselves through their capacity for labour (whether inside or outside of the home), as part of the economic structure of the family.[8] Representatives of state power, however, such as social workers or teachers, largely view working-class children according to their distance from middle class structures of family life.

To return once more to colonial India, we can see the ways in which children's sexuality was not only a marker of sexual modernity but a way of making racial hygiene into a moral project. British colonial elites conceived of their own children as innocent and in need of protection, both social and legal, but native children were a different matter entirely. As such, the question of childhood innocence became a key fault line in anticolonial nationalism. In the late 1800s, Indian reformers campaigned against the early marriage of girls, as the poor treatment of Indian women served as a key rationale for colonial rule – white men saving brown women from brown men. Prior to this, with the Indian Penal Code of 1860, the colonial government had set ten years as the age of consent for sexual consummation with girl children, whether married or unmarried. It should be noted that the Code outlawed only sex – and not marriage – with girl children below the age of ten. Seeking to revise this, some reformers' efforts resulted in the Special Marriage Act III of 1872, which instituted, among other things, a minimum age of marriage of fourteen for girls and eighteen for boys.

This legislation stirred public debate about child marriage among Hindus and led to the intensification of pleas for national reform.

The colonial government was reluctant to intervene, as state involvement in Hindu law went against the promise of 'non-interference'. Although reformers attempted to refute British doubts by claiming that child marriage was not in accordance with Hindu scriptures, revivalist-nationalists, who were against reforms, claimed the exact opposite. As such, the sexuality of children has been the source of continued debate, standing as a marker of racial difference and nationalist pride.

It is within this longer history of the child that we can start to understand the ways in which appeals to childhood innocence and vulnerability played out in the No Outsiders controversy. The parents framed their opposition to the curriculum through the slogan 'let kids be kids', asserting that LGBT RSE threatened to sexualise and confuse their children by introducing them to ideas 'unsuitable' for young minds. One might argue that the protestors were attempting to conserve their familial authority – their right to determine and protect the 'innocence' of their children – in the face of what they viewed as state intrusion into their moral autonomy. Of course, we cannot lose sight of the fact that their objection to the curriculum was homophobic and transphobic – that much is incontestable – but this fact must be considered within the larger tensions between state institutions and the family in determining the meaning of childhood, tensions which are particularly volatile when they run along racial lines.

In the public discourse about the protests, many LGBT people drew on their own childhoods to assert their concern about the protests, which touched a nerve for many whose school days had been endured under the shadow of state-sanctioned homophobia. Section 28 of the Local Government Act, which came into force in 1988 and was repealed in 2003, mandated that local authorities must not 'promote the teaching in any maintained school of the acceptability of homosexuality as a pretended family relationship'. A flood of articles detailed painful stories of teachers turning a blind eye to gay-bashing, educations disrupted, and the long aftermath of suffering caused by playground homophobia.[9] These stories were poignant and compelling, framed as the human toll that could be wrought once again if these protests were to be successful in their aims. Yet the suggestion that they marked a return to the dark days of Section 28 was a peculiar one; had it been subject to any clear-eyed scrutiny, it would likely have been dismissed as unlikely and misplaced. Indeed, given that, against the backdrop of these protests, the Conservative government passed legislation extending the requirements to teach LGBT issues in schools, the direction of travel seems to be away from Section 28 and towards a more gay-friendly set of policies regarding education and sexuality. A more urgent concern might have been why this new enthusiasm for LGBT RSE was being proclaimed by the most authoritarian and nationalist government in recent memory.

Instead, liberal LGBT objections to the protest focussed on the individual injury children would suffer. The isolation and marginal-isation LGBT adults felt as children under Section 28 was most effectively mobilised by queer Muslims, who were regularly plat-formed across media outlets. As Abeera Khan argues, 'Common themes cut across these narratives: they tend to address the potential psychic harm of the protests for students who may be LGBT+; there are recurring observations that LGBT+ Muslims would have benefited from programmes like No Outsiders during their own childhoods; and they often stress the need for a programme like No Outsiders in Muslim communities'.[10] The widespread recruitment of 'Muslim voices' by media outlets signalled a new racial politics that has learnt the lessons of a denuded intersectionality, viewing the 'queer Muslim' as the authentic voice of political truth. That these figures made no mention of the Prevent programme within which the curriculum had been conceived served to further obscure the wider context in which these relatively small protests became a national spectacle.

## Moral Panic

*Power defends itself by claiming a fragile, vulnerable group needs its protection from the savage hordes*

Barnaby Raine

Given that across the country, many small protests happen every day, and many parents pull their children out of RSE classes every week, we must ask why the protests in Birmingham became such a focus of national (and international) attention. Arguably, the No Outsiders controversy became a moral panic, condensing a series of social crises into a clear enemy. As the protests took hold, Britain was in the midst of the interminable Brexit impasse. The surprise victory of the Leave vote in the 2016 referendum on EU membership left the Tory party in a state of flux; authoritarian and isolationist tendencies were on the rise, emboldened by the referendum and the rehabilitation of aggressively nationalist rhetoric; more restrained, business-oriented and pro-European elements retained significant power within the party and sought a less decisive exit from the Union. Further, at the helm was the beleaguered and ineffective prime minister, Theresa May. May's virulent anti-immigrant politics from her days as home secretary remained, but her air of competence and certainty had been dramatically undermined by the surge of Corbynism in the 2017 election, which saw her lose the Conservative majority and forced into a coalition with the Democratic Unionist Party. Corbyn's campaign centred on social welfare, promising an end to the austerity policies which had drastically reduced living standards through defunding public services and cutting benefits.

While the underfunding of benefits and social care had been at the forefront of public discourse around austerity, education had also been subject to massive funding cuts and significant reorganisation, with the shift from locally run schools to academies forming the central plank of government education policy. Though academies continued to be state-funded, they are managed by not-for-profit private trusts, governed by company law, and answerable to the

Department of Education rather than the local authority. Academisation weakened the ties between schools and local authorities under the rubric of parental control over education, which strengthened precisely the 'parental rights' discourse on which the protestors staked their claim. As part of the same reorganisation of education, huge cuts to school budgets had also eroded parents' trust in the school system. In 2018, Anderton Park began to close early on Wednesday afternoons because dwindling funds meant the school couldn't afford to run for a full five days each week. As a result, pupils were deprived of lessons and parents had to arrange for extra childcare. Austerity, then, offers some measure of explanation for this moral panic. When protests began at Parkfield and Anderton Park (both academies), there was no mediating body between the schools and the Department for Education. Both the Brexit vote and these protests must be seen in the context of austerity, as well as placed within the longer history of British nationalism.

At the time of the protests, May was floundering in the Brexit negotiations and seen as out of her depth. She was unable to negotiate the terms of a deal that would be able to gain the backing of a sufficient number of MPs in an increasingly divided and volatile party. Being forced to delay the UK's withdrawal from the EU in this period was seen as a significant defeat and another example of May's incompetence. Whispers of a leadership contest, perhaps one in which Boris Johnson might prevail, were a constant feature of the first half of the year. In April 2019, in the midst of the Brexit chaos, parliament passed new regulations for teaching Relationships and Sex Education (RSE) in England. The legislation meant that from September 2020, all secondary schools in England were required to teach RSE, and all primary schools in England were required to teach Relationships Education (RE). The legislation passed with overwhelming support, thus giving the appearance of competence and power.

This illusion was especially useful to a flailing government, trying to manage the rifts of Brexit and unable to pass much in the way of meaningful legislation, having lost their majority. As Jyoti Puri notes in the Indian context, the regulation of matters of sexuality becomes particularly crucial in periods in which 'states are seen to be

diminishing due to the erosion of public services, the relentless drive
to privatize, the ubiquity of market-based logics that are exacerbated
by transnational flows of capital, and the pressures of transnational
political structures'.[11] By passing this RSE legislation, particularly in
the face of the protests held by the folk devil of the homophobic
Muslim parents, the state was able to confirm that it could take action
after all.

As the government benefited from successfully passing the legislation, so too did it profit from the distraction provided by the moral
panic. 'Brexit fatigue' had become a kind of shorthand for a national
polity in terminal decline, unable to enact even that which had been
decided upon by plebiscite, and lacking in coherence or conviction.
The protests displaced Brexit from the top of the news agenda by
deploying precisely the images that had helped to secure the vote to
leave the European Union in the first place. The Brexit vote had been
propelled by the juxtaposition of two images – the image of mostly
Muslim migrants at the borders of Europe under the caption 'Breaking
Point' in a 'Vote Leave' campaign poster; and that of a bus emblazoned
with the promise that leaving the EU would free up £350 million per
week to fund the NHS. The images worked together to imply that the
social safety net had been torn by the presence of racialised outsiders –
and that leaving the EU would restore public services (a metonym for
national dignity) to their rightful constituents. The return of this drama
of public services threatened by crowds of Muslims was given a powerful alibi by its new homonationalist articulation.

## Birmingham

*There are actual cities like Birmingham that are totally Muslim where
non-Muslims just simply don't go in.*

Bobby Jindal

David Cameron's 2015 speech on extremism – a kind of sequel to the
2011 'muscular liberalism' speech discussed in chapter 6 – was one
of the key sites of his promotion of this kind of virulent and targeted

homonationalism.[12] The speech was given at Ninestiles School in Birmingham. Birmingham was in the process of becoming a key site of Islamophobic fantasy in the national, and even international, imagination. In 2014, the 'Trojan horse' scandal emerged, claiming that Birmingham schools were being taken over by Islamic extremists. In January 2015, American Republican Bobby Jindal said that areas of Birmingham were a 'no-go zone' for non-Muslims. Though lambasted for his comments (mocking memes were shared euphorically across social media), they were nonetheless indicative of the development of Britain's Islamophobic psychogeography as a node in an international network of nationalist fervour.

The 'Trojan horse' affair is of particular importance to understanding the No Outsiders controversy, as it demonstrated the possibility of making political capital out of the education of working-class Muslim children. The controversy centred on Park View School in Alum Rock, which had transformed from a struggling institution to one that ranked in the top 14 per cent of all schools in the country. A student quoted in a profile of Park View said, 'The stereotype about Alum Rock is that the boys become taxi drivers and the girls get pregnant, but we were showing that we were more than that'.[13] This young woman's assessment is particularly notable for the ways in which the school might appear to be engaged in the kind of educational work that multiple governments have proposed is necessary for the 'integration' of Muslim communities.

Yet despite this tremendous academic success, the school became the target of an elaborate conspiracy theory, claiming it was at the centre of a plot to 'Islamicise' schools in Birmingham and beyond. One of the accusations laden with brutal irony was that the school had played extremist propaganda to its pupils. In fact, pupils had been shown a Panorama documentary by the local police as part of the school's adherence to the Prevent strategy. Many of the other allegations concerned matters of gender and sexuality: there was talk of 'morality squads', inadequate sex education provision, and gender segregation. Though the initial letter sent to Birmingham City Council that sparked the furore was quickly debunked and all litigation fell apart, this vicious conspiracy theory has nonetheless lived a long life. Many teachers had their names dragged through the mud and their careers ruined, students had to push past the press to take their exams, and the working-class Muslim community in Alum Rock found themselves demonised in the national and international press. Further, as John Holmwood and Therese O'Toole have elaborated, though the Trojan horse plot had no basis in fact, it has nonetheless been used to extend counterterrorism architecture further into the everyday lives of suspect populations.[14]

Referring to the Trojan horse affair in his 2015 speech, Cameron made it clear that he had come to Birmingham precisely because of its recent scandals. What Cameron did not mention was that the school at which he was speaking was attended by the son of Moazzam Begg, the British citizen who was detained without charge in Bagram prison and at Guantanamo Bay for three years but has never been charged with a crime. Further, Begg was the director of Cage (formerly Cageprisoners), an organisation that has been subject to continual repressive attacks by the British government, including the freezing of its bank accounts and assets. Cameron directly referred to Cage in his speech, making an implicit attack on a child sitting in the room. We should view the No Outsiders controversy within a longer history that has tentacles that span the globe but which pass more than once through Birmingham.

## Convergences and Contradictions

*The reported clash of opposites is actually a family feud.*

Quinn Slobodian

We might see the No Outsiders controversy as a kind of transitional space in which we can see the old paradigm become the new. In the focus on Muslim parents – the bad, backwards homophobes – the emergence of a wider, more peculiar right-wing ecology was obscured. In the response to the protests by the school, the police, the women's sector, and the media, we saw the right to assembly demonised, clearing the deck for the increasingly draconian legislation on protest that has emerged since 2019. In the response of Southall Black Sisters, a domestic violence organisation that was involved in antiracist struggles in the 1980s, we can trace the ways in which certain figures from the New Left have found themselves increasingly aligned with state interventions into communities with whom they may have, at an earlier moment, sought to build an alliance.

This relentless focus on the imagined queer child in 2019 offered a glimpse of what was to come – namely, the use of the child as a node around which heterogenous groups with divergent political interests might coalesce to make momentary, often bizarre, alliances. There have been many attempts to understand this trend. It encompasses the incel and MRA subcultures described in the previous chapter, alongside anti-vaccine and anti-lockdown movements against public health measures in response to the Covid-19 pandemic, as well as New Age spiritualities and various conspiracy theories. William Callison and Quinn Slobodian refer to this new political modality as 'diagonalism', taking their cue from the Querdenken movement in Germany.[15] While 'querdenken' translates to 'thinking outside of the box', the movement is emblematic of a new, inchoate political modality which encompasses both fascistic and more libertarian tendencies.

Though the new 'diagonal' politics are highly invested in the individual, the familiar forms of self-realisation promised by sexual modernity are more muted and there is no clearly defined set of political values holding this unstable coalition together. In many ways, however, this is the movement's strength and the source of its momentum. Coalitions – both formal and informal – can come together briefly around particular flashpoints. In the case of the No Outsiders controversy, a range of different characters took on prominent roles, brokering alliances between the groups they were taken to represent. In this final section, I'll work through some of these characters and the alliances they formed.

As mentioned earlier in this chapter, teacher and researcher Andrew Moffat became a household name through his promotion of the curriculum. Moffat led Birmingham's pride parade in the summer of 2019, and was joined by local Muslim LGBT activists Khakan

Qureshi and Saima Razzaq. They too became prominent figures, called upon to provide an 'authentic' queer Muslim voice. Though No Outsiders was the result of a collective research project, it quickly became a recognisable 'brand' with Moffat as its face. Moffat was widely interviewed, including on independent left platforms such as Owen Jones's YouTube channel, as well as on right-leaning daytime television. Notably, despite longstanding involvement in antiracist activism, Owen Jones offered no challenge to the ways in which the curriculum was conceived of as a way to promote 'British Values' within the government's counterterrorism agenda, and Moffat simply repeated the usual talking points about equality and inclusion. The relative absence of critique or contextualisation from queer left-wing quarters was particularly stark given the widespread circulation of Puar's coinage of 'homonationalism'. Faced with the frightening images of religious and racialised homophobia and its perceived threat to the promise of sexual modernity, the queer community mostly retreated into the grooves of gay liberalism.

Southall Black Sisters (SBS) also played a curious role, collaborating with a local LGBT group in Birmingham to put on an event in support of the school. SBS were instrumental to antiracist feminism in the 1980s, in particular by supporting South Asian survivors of domestic violence. They are also closely aligned with Women Against Fundamentalism and have increasingly found themselves in collaboration with the UK government's Islamophobic policies rather than, as in the 1980s, opposing state racism.[16] Given this context, it may seem unsurprising that they took on a prominent role in opposing the protests, which they viewed as an example of religious extremism. Yet, on a closer look, another contradiction is lodged within their involvement. In recent years, as trans politics have gained political traction, SBS have formed alliances with key parts of the reactionary movement of organised transphobia. They have, for example, expressed support for A Woman's Place, arguably the most well-known transphobic feminist group in the UK.[17] Given their hostility to trans people, it's notable that SBS decided to express such active support for a trans-positive curriculum. It is not inconceivable that, in another context, SBS could find themselves on the other side of the debate.

Anderton Park's headteacher, Sarah Hewitt-Clarkson, expressed frustration, claiming that freedom of assembly (which she referred to as a 'great British law') was causing significant problems.[18] Her comments are particularly resonant in the context of the Brexit negotiations that were ongoing at the time. Brexit had, in part, been propelled by the belief that the European Union was imposing human rights norms on Britain to which its own citizens did not subscribe. As such, the suggestion that the right to assembly was 'causing a problem' takes on a sharp nationalist resonance.

Finally, at the heart of the protests was Shakeel Afsar, a young property developer and landlord from Birmingham and the uncle of children at Anderton Park school. Though not a parent, he became the de facto leader of the protests, giving speeches, speaking to the media, and quickly becoming a recognisable face and name, despite having no previous public profile. Khakan Qureshi observed that Afsar had 'the gift of the gab' and as the protests wore on, many observed that they had become 'the Shakeel show', with other parents increasingly alienated from the spectacle despite their continued opposition to LGBT RSE.[19] Afsar could be seen as one of the 'freelance media hustlers, movement messiahs, and entrepreneurial contrarians' that Callison and Slobodian observe as playing key roles in the new diagonal politics.[20] In this vein, Afsar was happy to make bizarre and disturbing alliances, including with far-right media personality Katie Hopkins. Hopkins has styled herself as a key figure in the far-right media ecology, using her high profile as a columnist for *The Sun* to promote the racist conspiracy theory of 'white genocide', referring to migrants as cockroaches and calling on people to fight against Muslims. The alliance between Hopkins and Afsar is suggestive of the ways in which issues of gender and sexuality can be used to recruit racialised minorities into the orbit of a virulent, aggressive nationalism.

## Contract and Conspiracy

*A once-in-a-lifetime opportunity to take this global cabal of Satan-worshipping paedophiles out.*

> Marjorie Taylor Greene, the leading candidate in the race for
> Georgia's fourteenth congressional district seat, on QAnon

As many of the tenets of sexual modernity are shifting, the particular position of children – as repositories of innocence, hope, and possibility – is being strengthened. According to Julia O'Connell Davidson, the obsession with childhood as a position of inherent innocence (rather than a constructed position of social subordination) comes down to a set of anxieties about the role of contract in determining freedom.[21] As I have explored throughout this book, the operation of power rarely announces itself as such. Though racism excludes, marginalises, and kills, it also cajoles, convinces, and seduces. As I explored in chapter 4, contract and consent were crucial to the development of liberal ideas of freedom, through which people would be made responsible for their own choices, regardless of the context in which these were made. This logic became particularly stark as neoliberalism hit its apotheosis as a governing rationality, as I described in chapter 5 regarding New Labour's punitive approach to those who refused to take on the 'contract' of romantic love and the couple form.

As O'Connell Davidson explains, the 'freedom' of contract 'becomes its own burden, its own anti-freedom'. As such 'children, who are socially constructed as beyond or outside contract, promise a refuge from this existential horror, at least so long as we can be certain of their fundamental difference from ourselves. Thus, we cherish the innocence, dependency, helplessness, and asexuality of "the child", and rage against the paedophile who defiles it'.[22] This rage against the paedophile is, of course, a tabloid staple, with moral panics about 'stranger danger' and child molesters lurking in the shadows deflecting from the more common experience of sexual violence incubated within the family. This investment in children as existing outside of the structures of contract and consent is so power-fully hegemonic that, in the No Outsiders controversy, both the protestors and the proponents of the curriculum viewed the other as defiling the moral innocence of children – of drawing them into the adult world of choice.

In the last few years, narratives of child sexual exploitation have taken on a new lease of life. The 'Pizzagate' conspiracy theory, which had gained traction on right-wing social media channels, came to wider public attention when, in December 2016, a man fired an assault rifle in the Comet Ping Pong restaurant in Washington, DC, in response to the conspiracy theory that liberal political operatives were running a child-sex-trafficking ring from the basement of the DC pizzeria. This conspiracy theory was foundational to the development of QAnon, according to which this cabal of paedophiles (now also Satanists and perhaps cannibals) can only be stopped by Donald Trump. If we return to the moral panic about 'grooming gangs', the racialising potential of this obsession with childhood becomes clear. Figures such as Tommy Robinson and Nick Griffin have used what they refer to as 'rape jihad gangs' as a means to rebuild and sustain their fanbases, drawing in an audience to their social media channels, videos, and other kinds of online content. They claim 'grooming gangs' are facilitated by the liberal elites who sought to overturn the democratic vote to leave the EU, suturing together Brexit, the sexual exploitation of children, and the dignity of English masculinity. One can see in this process a prototype for what Seymour has called QAnon's 'conversion machine' which 'converts non-believers into believers'.[23]

If we consider the case of Darren Osborne, who ploughed a van into worshippers at Finsbury Park Mosque, leading to the death of Makram Ali and injuring nine other worshippers, it becomes clear that a pathway into these digital subcultures can be found through legacy media. Osborne became obsessed with the BBC drama *Three Girls* and its depiction of the sexual abuse of young white women and girls in Rochdale. After watching the drama, he sought out fellow travellers online, watching videos of Tommy Robinson and other far-right hucksters. He told his partner that Muslims were 'raping children and . . . blowing people up'.[24] It's clear from his actions that he had a visceral response to the story of the 'grooming gangs'; he felt claimed, called, interpolated by the Islamophobic narrative. In avenging these crimes, he thought his own sense of self would be restored.

In her work on children in the global sex trade, O'Connell Davidson observes that though many people seem highly motivated to stop the sexual abuse of children, the other ways in which young people come to harm fails to attract significant attention. The fact that 'there are children in the world who are malnourished, without access to clean water, dying from preventable diseases, exploited in sweatshops and on plantations, and so on' is largely viewed with a kind of equanimity. The promise of sexual modernity – of self-realisation through romantic love and the couple form – has little to offer in the face of the degradations of capitalism. Even the horizon of sexual experimentation and authentic gender expression is paltry compensation for diminishing living standards and limited autonomy in every other area of our lives.

Implicit in concerns around organised sexual exploitation is the painful realisation that the nuclear family can do little to protect children from abuse, not least because the nuclear family itself so often incubates sexual violence. In this context, the rewards are great for those who can claim to offer stability, certainty, and dignity. Nationalist formations around the world are capitalising on these desires and using the ecstatic and contagious possibilities of social media to convert sceptics into believers, engagement into capital, and loose affiliations into effective political networks. As movements against public health restrictions grow at an alarming rate in the teeth of the Covid-19 pandemic, the influence of conspiracy theory on matters of statecraft is becoming apparent. While it may be too early to make definitive predictions, it seems clear that these emergent formations will play a role in the development of new racial orders.

# Coda:
# The Promise that Would Never Be Kept

In *Castes of Mind: Colonialism and the Making of Modern India*, Nicholas Dirks seeks to understand what he refers to as the 'special perversity of colonial modernity', the way in which imperialism asserts a moral project that is sullied from the very beginning by its deadly production of racial difference. As Dirks observes, 'The colonizer held out modernity as a promise but at the same time made it the limiting condition of coloniality: the promise that would never be kept. The colonized could be seduced by the siren of the modern but never quite get there, mired necessarily (if colonialism was to continue to legitimate itself) in a "traditional" world'.[1] In these final pages, I would like to suggest that the siren song of the modern is not only an illusion for those racialised Others held to be trapped in modernity's shadows, but is, for all, a promise that will never be kept. The faltering promise of sexual modernity, even for those who conform to its scripts, coheres with a shift in Britain's racial regime. Racism's legitimating fictions are increasingly contested. Meanwhile, the practices of statecraft which make some groups vulnerable to premature death become ever more virulent.

In this book, we've seen the ways in which the making of race is both intentional and chaotic; categories are slippery and dynamic, yet curiously durable. By returning both empire and gender to the story, we have been able to glimpse that which is absent from Foucault's account. Not only do the gaps in his analysis obscure the production of racial categories, they also make it difficult to fully grasp the relationship between biopolitics and capitalism. As Maria Mies reminds us, 'not only domestic labour of women all over the world was "a free resource" for capital, but also the work of small peasants and that of slum-dwellers in the cities. The same was/is true for colonies and particularly for nature. For capitalists, all these are "colonies" whose production can be appropriated almost free of costs.[2] By attending to the historical context in which sexual modernity takes hold, we can start to understand the way in which accumulation by dispossession depended on categorisation – on determining that which could (and should) be extracted or exploited. As Nancy Fraser argues, however, capitalism's 'orientation to endless accumulation threatens to destabilize these very conditions of its possibility'.[3] Holding out the promise of sexual modernity while punishing those excluded from its gains is an attempt to stabilise the chaos wrought by capitalism. But the forms of statecraft involved in race-making bring complex and contradictory consequences.

While the discussion of British governance in colonial India has necessarily been brief – whole libraries are needed to document and understand colonial governance – even a few examples reveal the elaborate work needed to secure foreign rule over a vast subcontinent. By drawing out the Möbius strip of culture and sexuality, I have tried to show the ways in which empire relied upon careful gradations of status as firmly as it did on ships and canons. The hierarchy of race cannot be understood alone, especially not in South Asia, where all social relations are crosshatched by caste and religion. In revealing the work of sexuality in maintaining these gradations of power, I hope to have contributed to our collective understanding of what makes these complex social fictions endure. Further, in following race-making from empire to nation-state, innovations are as important as continuities. By showing the ways in which sexual modernity and racial governance shifts, we can see that racial regimes are incoherent, founded as they are on a brutal premise. It is crucial that we attend to this incoherence, to the irrationality of race, for this is a weakness that antiracists can exploit. Further, as we can see in the innovations of the War on Terror, forms of statecraft initially tested on denigrated racial Others will likely capture many more in their net.

While the state's capacity to preserve or support the nuclear family and the couple form is increasingly thinning, the biopolitical imperative to make live and let die has not disappeared – it remains the preserve of the nation-state project. We see the state's command over life and death in police killings in working-class neighbourhoods, in the stratification of mortality rates in the Covid-19 pandemic; in the deaths of migrants in the English Channel. The British government's response to Covid-19 was a particularly acute reminder that, though the language of eugenics discussed in chapter 2 is now muted, its logic is much harder to dislodge. While it was clear that matters of labour and housing were at the root of the racial disparities in Covid-19 deaths, biology and culture were regularly cited as factors, with the overrepresentation of Asian families living in multigenerational households viewed in cultural, rather than economic, terms.

The acts of violence or neglect through which the state sanctions premature death for certain populations continue. But the cruelty, exploitation, and murderous indifference that forms the material basis of the racial order is increasingly visible as the work of securing something altogether less seductive than the promise of sexual modernity. As living standards plummet, the family is under increasing strain, unable to carry the burden of care with rising prices and crumbling state support. No more can the political order convincingly claim to be acting to protect the glittering offer of self-realisation, romantic love, sexual adventure, and reliable care from racialised outsiders who lurk in the shadows. The capitalist social relations that produced the nuclear family and couple form have also generated the conditions for them to be undermined. The attendant language of meritocracy, described in chapter 5, now rings hollow. As a result, nation-state formations can demand loyalty and obedience in return only for ensuring that racial Others are worse off. In the British context, this horizon of negative solidarity needs to be constantly renewed by stories of aggrieved and innocent white natives at the mercy of powerful conspiracies.

It is in the context of state neglect, capitalist crisis, and ecological breakdown that we must situate the fractures in sexual modernity and the new nationalisms that are growing in its place. Many of the developments I have explored in part II are attempts to shore up sexual modernity, to give it the flexibility to withstand the winds of change. New Labour's embrace of gay rights and punitive approach to single mothers, for example, was an attempt to construct a flexible workforce who could respond to the changing dynamics of the global market. In doing so, they shifted the emphasis towards romantic love and the couple form as a *choice*, one that aligned with modern, progressive values. The idea of an 'identity crisis', explored in chapter 6, relies upon the idea that racialised forms of kinship (the extended family, the gang, the religious community) threaten romantic love – and in turn pose a risk to the individual, and the nation. As such, new regimes of punishment and exclusion are justified in the name of sexual modernity.

In chapter 7, we saw how the figure of the Jihadi bride sparks such vitriol precisely because she turns away from the promise of self-realisation in its accepted form, instead using her agency in service to other aims, electing for an arranged marriage within a strict religious community. The Jihadi bride finds a correlate in the rise of the incel, a figure who embraces the implicit hierarchies of sexual modernity, even as he feels marginalised by its brutal Social Darwinism. In chapter 8, we saw the ways in which the figure of the child as a sexual innocent offers a point of certainty around which new nationalist formations can build power. These 'inchoate fascisms'[4] are multiracial, drawing a broader range of subjects into their orbit and brokering new alliances across unstable racial orders. In these final two chapters, we saw that though the techniques of the racial state – exclusion, incarceration, abandonment and so on – intensify, their justificatory mythology is thinner and less potent. As marriage and the nuclear family fail to protect us from capitalist crises, viral threats, lowering living standards, and the incursions of state power into our intimate lives and bodily autonomy, sexual modernity's story of the good life lacks conviction.

In this context, feminist and queer critiques of sexual respectability and the gender binary have found a large and sympathetic audience. As Chitty points out, however, although this ongoing crisis of modern sexual categories may initially have produced a utopian sense that societies were moving beyond rigid binary systems, such celebrations of intransitivity have missed the ways in which gender and sexual flexibility have also been forced upon subjects as a consequence of precarity.[5]

While Chitty's statement might be provocative, we must nonetheless be highly suspicious of openings in personal expression that are wholly severed from more collective forms of care. Freedom from the gender binary and from the demands of monogamy or the nuclear family can only be a Pyrrhic victory if offered as compensation for dwindling access to the means of life. Further, as Jordy Rosenberg has argued, 'today's neofascism . . . has a strange, parasitic relationship to the energies of the family's decomposition'.[6] As the nuclear family and couple form lose their protective capacities, established and insurgent nationalisms compete to take control of the conceptual space vacated by the old promises.

As the long decomposition of the former certainties of gender and kinship accelerates, so too does a growing unease with liberal multiculturalism. The liberal view of Britain's racial Others as tolerable curiosities – at least once their stubborn attachments to sexual backwardness have been loosened by the civilising interventions of a benign nation-state – now appears anachronistic. A more explicit authoritarian nationalism competes with an incipient antiracism that is highly sceptical of state power. The shift towards this authoritarian nationalism has been propelled by racial ressentiment; the campaign to leave the EU, for example, was premised on the notion that living standards were falling for deserving white Britons while migrants were given a free ride, living it up on the state's dime. The tide of racist violence unleashed by the Brexit vote has taken both institutional and street-based forms.

Waves of unruly racist attacks, in public space and on social media, dovetail with draconian legislation which extends the state's arsenal of detention, surveillance, and deportation. The Nationality and Borders Act criminalises anyone helping someone seeking asylum to enter the UK, regardless of whether their help is for financial gain.

This includes criminalising the Royal National Lifeboat Institution for rescuing asylum seekers at risk of drowning. The Police, Crime, Sentencing and Courts Act is similarly broad, seeking to criminalise mass protest – precisely the spaces in which forms of collectivity take hold. This new legislation sets its sights on solidarity – on the bonds of love, intimacy, and connection that the family can never contain.

Though the illusory promise of sexual modernity is giving way, we must not turn away too soon from its underbelly. Along with premature death and widespread suffering, the vagaries of capitalist development also incubate sexual violence and exploitation. The case of the 'grooming gangs' we encountered in the second half of the book offers a useful counterpoint to the forms of sexual exploitation that attend military occupation and extractive industries. To reiterate the example explored in chapter 3, the influx of workers, soldiers, administrators, and merchants who arrived in India to accumulate raw materials and manage the unruly masses led to state-regulated sex work. And to maintain suitable brothels for English soldiers, separate from those used by native men, the colonial authorities could arrest, detain, and conduct forced genital inspections on all Indian women, regardless of their profession. As such, the extraction of labour and resources brought widespread sexual violation.

But the flight of capital can have a similar impact. As discussed in chapter 6, the organised sexual exploitation that has come to travel under the sign of the 'grooming gang' largely took place in deindustrialised towns where the demise of industry radically disorganised the social terrain. Earlier in the book, I offered a critique of the ways in which the retelling of these events has become a racial story, used to widen the use of citizenship stripping and deportation, as well as to rebuild the ranks of the far-right. In these final pages, I'd like to underline the ways in which both the flood of capital and its retreat can alter the social relations of particular locations, with stark consequences borne differently according to race, class, and gender. The impersonal forces of capitalism unleash sexual violence, as well as other forms of degradation, and these often become organised along and across precisely the racial lines that undergird regimes of economic exploitation.

Crises of accumulation, the retreat of state agencies, and the prevalence of low-waged, gig economy work are accelerating: sexual violence will likely follow. Unless a more militant and grounded feminism intervenes, reactionary forces may attempt to follow the rhetorical playbook used in the case of 'grooming gangs'. As we saw in the No Outsiders controversy, sexual scandals retain some capacity to condense wider political crises into moral panics. But the terrain is increasingly crowded and a range of political actors seek to capitalise on the confusion, sometimes forming new and unpredictable alliances in the process. While these may not always run along familiar racial lines, they nonetheless remain freighted with the sedimented and dangerous logic of race-thinking. As such, the notion that the racial Other is a sexual deviant retains its power, even as the racial order and the acts or desires considered deviant might change.

When insurgent and established nationalisms seek to cannibalise modernity's decomposing forms, it is tempting to view the old certainties – the family, the welfare state – with a certain nostalgia. Instead, we must think anew about the violence done in the name of sexual freedom, the illicit sexual connections it both produces and criminalises, and the racial order it fortifies. Here we can follow the example of anticolonial thinkers, who have always insisted that race-thinking damaged the coloniser as well as the colonised. Perhaps then we'll see more clearly that even for those in whose name the promise of sexual modernity was made, it has never been kept.

# Acknowledgements

Writing this book has been a long process and one that I would neither have started nor finished without the help of many people.

I worked through the first iteration of these ideas during my PhD at King's College London, during which the intellectual support of Paul Gilroy as a supervisor was invaluable. Thanks to Verso, and especially to my editor, Rosie Warren, for taking on the book and giving me the opportunity to take these ideas in a new direction. My enormous gratitude to Manjari Sahay for highly skilled research assistance, with chapter 3 in particular.

Colleagues and comrades at King's College London have been a huge source of support – thanks to Seb Franklin, Amy De'ath, Luke Roberts, Jane Elliott, and Clare Birchall for helping me through my first proper academic job. A special thanks goes to Jane whose remarkable insights into the general chaos of the world have helped me to navigate it in recent years.

A huge thank you to the RICE family – Adam Elliott-Cooper, Dalia Gebrial, Gargi Bhattacharyya, Kerem Nişancıoğlu, Kojo Koram, Luke de Noronha, and Nadine El-Enany. Working on *Empire's Endgame* with such an insightful, hilarious, comradely crew helped to renew my enthusiasm for thinking and writing.

I feel very lucky to have friends flung far and wide who have my back. A big thank you to Caoimhe Mader McGuinness, Elise Eisenkraft Klein, Evelina Gambino, Fuad Musallam, Jay Bernard, Kathryn

Maude, Mumbi Nkonde, Nazmia Jamal, Melissa Rakshana Steiner, Sara Sassanelli, and Zinzi Minott.

Thank you to Anne-Marie Stewart, Bekah Sparrow, Latifa Akay, and Nadine El-Enany, who offered tremendously useful insights on earlier draft chapters. I'm grateful for your patient and attentive reading skills and even more so for the many conversations that have helped to shape my ideas over the years. I am eternally grateful to Luke de Noronha, whose generosity and insight as a friend, reader, and intellectual comrade helped to get the book over the line.

The quiet encouragement of my family has helped to keep me going. Didi, thank you for always being on my team. Ma, your hard work is the reason this book exists. Dad, watching you discover that you're a writer has both inspired and fortified me.

Finally, Nisha Eswaran. For nudging me to keep going and for helping me to take breaks. For reading every word and talking through every idea. For the sharpest edits and kindest suggestions. For loving me even when I'm a huge pain. For being my compadre in everything. Thank you.

# Notes

## Introduction

1. Cedric J. Robinson, *Forgeries of Memory and Meaning: Blacks and the Regimes of Race in American Theater and Film before World War II*, Chapel Hill: University of North Carolina Press, 2007, 4.
2. Ruth Wilson Gilmore, *Golden Gulag: Prisons, Surplus, Crisis, and Opposition in Globalizing California*, Berkeley: University of California Press, 2006, 28.
3. Ian Patel, *We're Here Because You Were There: Immigration and the End of Empire*, London: Verso Books, 2021, 5.
4. Toni Morrison, 'Race Matters', in *Mouth Full of Blood: Essays, Speeches, Meditations*, London: Vintage, 2020, 133.
5. Robinson, *Forgeries of Memory*, xii.
6. Michel Foucault, *Society Must Be Defended: Lectures at the Collège De France, 1975–76*, trans. David Macey, New York: Picador, 2003, 258.
7. David Theo Goldberg, *The Racial State*, Oxford: Blackwell Publishers, 2002, 104.
8. Radhika Viyas Mongia, 'Race, Nationality, Mobility: A History of the Passport', in *After The Imperial Turn*, ed. Antoinette Burton, Durham: Duke University Press, 2003, 529.
9. Gargi Bhattacharyya, *Crisis, Austerity, and Everyday Life: Living in a Time of Diminishing Expectations*, Basingtoke: Palgrave Macmillan, 2015, 28.
10. Etienne Balibar, 'Racism and Nationalism', in *Race, Nation, Class*, ed. Balibar and Immanuel Wallerstein, London: Verso, 1991, 54.
11. Kimberlé Crenshaw, 'Mapping the Margins: Intersectionality, Identity Politics, and Violence against Women of Color', *Stanford Law Review*, 43 (1991), 1241–99.

12. Paul Gilroy, *The Black Atlantic: Modernity and Double-Consciousness*, London: Verso Books, 1993, 85.

13. See Martin Barker, *The New Racism*, London: Junction Books, 1981, for an early and influential account.

14. Rahul Rao, *Out of Time: The Queer Politics of Postcoloniality*, Oxford: Oxford University Press, 2020, 15.

15. Edward W. Said, *Orientalism*, New York: Knopf Doubleday Publishing Group, 2014, 40.

16. Nicholas B. Dirks, *Castes of Mind: Colonialism and the Making of Modern India*, Princeton: Princeton University Press, 2001, 44.

17. Ibid., 9.

18. Rao, *Out of Time*, 15.

19. T. B. Macaulay, 'Minute on Education', in *Sources of Indian Tradition: Modern India, and Pakistan, Volume 2*, ed. William Theodore de Bary, New York: Columbia University Press, 1958, 49.

20. Mahmood Mamdani, *Citizen and Subject: Contemporary Africa and the Legacy of Late Colonialism*, Princeton: Princeton University Press, 2018, 49.

21. Stuart Hall, 'Gramsci's Relevance for the Study of Race and Ethnicity', *Journal of Communication Inquiry* 10, 1986, 27.

22. Stuart Hall, and Alan O'Shea, 'Common-sense Neoliberalism', *Soundings* 5, 2013, 9.

23. Stuart Hall, and Les Back, 'At Home and Not at Home: Stuart Hall in Conversation with Les Back', *Cultural Studies* 23: 4, 2009.

24. Jasbir K. Puar, *Terrorist Assemblages: Homonationalism in Queer Times*, Durham: Duke University Press, 2007.

25. Lisa Duggan, *The Twilight of Equality?: Neoliberalism, Cultural Politics, and the Attack on Democracy*, Boston: Beacon Press, 2004.

26. Nat Raha, 'The Limits of Trans Liberalism', Verso Blog, 2015.

27. Cathy J. Cohen, 'Punks, Bulldaggers, and Welfare Queens: The Radical Potential of Queer Politics?' in *Black Queer Studies*, ed. E. Patrick Johnson and Mae G. Henderson, Durham: Duke University Press, 2005.

28. Olúfẹ́mi O. Táíwò, 'Being-in-the-Room Privilege: Elite Capture and Epistemic Deference', *The Philosopher*, 108 , 4, 2020.

29. Sylvia Wynter, 'Unsettling the Coloniality of Being/Power/Truth/Freedom: Towards the Human, after Man, Its Overrepresentation – An Argument', *CR: The New Centennial Review* 3: 3, 2003.

## 1 Sexual Modernity

1. Michel Foucault, *History of Sexuality: Volume 1*, trans. Richard Howard, New York: Pantheon, 1978, 154.
2. Ibid., 18.
3. Ibid., 19.
4. Quoted in Marshall Berman, *All That Is Solid Melts Into Air: The Experience of Modernity*, New York: Penguin Publishing Group, 1988, 75.
5. Charles Taylor, *The Ethics of Authenticity*, Cambridge: Harvard University Press, 1992, 26.
6. Gargi Bhattacharyya, *Dangerous Brown Men: Exploiting Sex, Violence and Feminism in the 'War on Terror'*, London: Bloomsbury Academic, 2008, 14.
7. Foucault, *History of Sexuality*, 38.
8. María Lugones, 'Heterosexualism and the Colonial/Modern Gender System', *Hypatia* 22: 1, 2007, 190.
9. Rahul Rao, 'Global Homocapitalism', *Radical Philosophy*, 194, 2015, 42.
10. Sylvia Federici, *Caliban and the Witch*, Brooklyn: Autonomedia, 2009, 97.
11. Matthew Carlin and Silvia Federici, 'The Exploitation of Women, Social Reproduction, and the Struggle against Global Capital', *Theory & Event* 17: 3, 2014.
12. David Harvey, *The New Imperialism*, Oxford: Oxford University Press, 2003.
13. National Inquiry into Missing and Murdered Indigenous Women and Girls, *Reclaiming Power and Place: The Final Report of the National Inquiry into Missing and Murdered Indigenous Women and Girls*, Ottawa: Government of Canada, 2019.
14. Brandi Morin, 'Pipelines, Man Camps and Murdered Indigenous Women in Canada', *Al Jazeera*, 5 May 2020.
15. Maya Oppenheim, 'Kenyan Woman Allegedly Murdered by British Soldier has Been Denied Justice "Because She was a Sex Worker",' *Independent*, 16 December 2021.
16. Nancy Fraser, 'Behind Marx's Hidden Abode', *New Left Review*, 64, 2014.
17. Carlin and Federici, 'The Exploitation of Women'.
18. Friedrich Engels, *The Origin of the Family, Private Property and the State*, London: Verso Books, 2021, 56.

19. Fraser, 'Behind Marx's Hidden Abode'.

20. Ann L. Stoler, *Race and the Education of Desire: Foucault's History of Sexuality and the Colonial Order of Things*, Durham: Duke University Press, 1995.

21. Christopher Chitty, *Sexual Hegemony: Statecraft, Sodomy, and Capital in the Rise of the World System*, Durham: Duke University Press, 2020.

22. Raymond Williams, *Marxism and Literature*, Oxford: Oxford University Press, 1977, 125.

23. See Nisha Eswaran, 'The Nation-State is Not Our Friend: On Celebrating the Repeal of Section 377', *Jamhoor*, November 2018, for an incisive critique of this articulation.

24. Rao, *Out of Time*, xix.

25. Quoted in Evan Smith and Marinella Marmo, *Race, Gender and the Body in British Immigration Control: Subject to Examination*, Basingstoke: Palgrave Macmillan, 2014, 152.

26. Quoted in Smith and Marmo, *Race, Gender and the Body*, 91.

27. Quoted in Elizabeth Kolsky, 'The Colonial Rule of Law and the Legal Regime of Exception: Frontier "Fanaticism" and State Violence in British India', *American Historical Review* 120: 4, 2015.

28. Said, *Orientalism*.

29. Quoted Smith and Marmo, *Race, Gender and the Body*, 89.

30. Radhika Mongia, 'Symposium on Radhika Mongia's *Indian Migration And Empire: A Colonial Genealogy of the Modern State*', *The Disorder of Things*, 18 February 2021, thedisorderofthings.com.

31. Quoted in Smith and Marmo, *Race, Gender and the Body*, 82.

## 2  Sexual Science

1. Jordan B. Peterson, *12 Rules for Life: An Antidote to Chaos*, London, Penguin Books, 2018.

2. Ibid., 28.

3. Ibid., 27.

4. Forthcoming.

5. Patrick Wolfe, *Traces of History: Elementary Structures of Race*, London: Verso Books, 2016, 202.

6. Michel Foucault, *The Order of Things*, London: Taylor & Francis, 2005, 61.

7. Ibid., 65.

8. Lennard J. Davis. *Enforcing Normalcy: Disability, Deafness, and the Body*, London: Verso, 1995, 25.

9. Thomas Laqueur, *Making Sex: Body and Gender from the Greeks to Freud*, Cambridge: Harvard University Press, 1992, 6.

10. Sylvia Wynter and David Scott, 'The Re-enchantment of Humanism: An Interview with Sylvia Wynter', *Small Axe* 8: 1, 2000, 120.

11. Foucault, *The Order of Things*, 137.

12. Georges-Louis Leclerc, Comte de Buffon, quoted in Londa Schiebinger, *Nature's Body: Gender in the Making of Modern Science*, Boston: Beacon Press, 1993, 28.

13. Greta LaFleur, *Natural History of Sexuality in the Early Americas*, Baltimore: Johns Hopkins University Press, 2020, 2.

14. Anne McClintock, *Imperial Leather: Race, Gender and Sexuality in the Colonial Contest*, Abingdon: Routledge, 1995, 39.

15. Schiebinger, *Nature's Body*, 12.

16. Lawrence Stone quoted in Schiebinger, *Nature's Body*, 87.

17. Schiebinger, *Nature's Body*, 26.

18. Patricia Fara, *Sex, Botany & Empire: The Story of Carl Linnaeus and Joseph Banks*, London: Icon, 2004, 405.

19. Laqueur, *Making Sex*, 149.

20. Schiebinger, *Nature's Body*, 55.

21. Banu Subramaniam, *Ghost Stories for Darwin: The Science of Variation and the Politics of Diversity*, Chicago: University of Illinois Press, 2014, 77.

22. Nancy Leys Stepan, 'Race and Gender: The Role of Analogy in Science', *Isis* 77: 2, 1986, 263.

23. Ibid., 263.

24. Ibid., 273.

25. Arvind-Pal Singh Mandair, 'The Unbearable Proximity of the Orient: Political Religion, Multiculturalism and the Retrieval of South Asian Identities', *Social Identities* 10: 5, 2004, 649.

26. Stepan, 'Race and Gender', 266.

27. Lugones, 'Heterosexualism', 186.

28. Hortense J. Spillers, 'Mama's Baby, Papa's Maybe: An American Grammar Book', *Diacritics* 17: 2, 1987, 65.

29. Subramaniam, *Ghost Stories for Darwin*, 50.

30. Ibid., 18.

31. Haggard quoted in McClintock, *Imperial Leather*, 51.
32. McClintock, *Imperial Leather*, 50.


## 3 Racial Hygiene

1. E. M. Forster, 'The Other Boat' in *The Life to Come and Other Stories*, New York: W.W. Norton and Company, 1972/1987.
2. Ibid., 171.
3. Ibid., 177.
4. Ibid., 171.
5. Ibid., 172.
6. Ibid., 171.
7. Ibid., 171.
8. Forms of racial hygiene, including sexual violence, can be found across the archives of European empires. The history of plantation slavery, for example, is one in which rape, racial distinctions, and sexual respectability are constantly intertwined. See Rachel A. Fernstein, *When Rape was Legal: The Untold History of Sexual Violence during Slavery*, New York: Routledge, 2018; Saidiya Hartman, 'The Belly of the World: A Note on Black Women's Labors', *Souls* 18: 1. 2016; Sandra C. Duvivier '"My Body Is My Piece of Land": Female Sexuality, Family, and Capital in Caribbean Texts', *Callaloo* 31: 4, 2008; Fred Moten, *In the Break: The Aesthetics of the Black Radical Tradition*, Minneapolis: University of Minnesota Press, 2003.
9. Mary Louise Pratt, 'Arts of the Contact Zone', *Profession* 1991, 34.
10. Peter Linebaugh and Marcus Rediker, *The Many-Headed Hydra*, London: Verso, 2012, 162.
11. McClintock, *Imperial Leather*, 56.
12. Lisa Lowe, 'The Intimacies of Four Continents', in *Haunted By Empire*, ed. Ann L. Stoler, Durham: Duke University Press, 2006, 195.
13. Said, *Orientalism*, 42.
14. Lowe, 'The Intimacies of Four Continents', 199.
15. Foucault, *History of Sexuality*, 124.
16. Stoler, *Race and the Education of Desire*, 14.
17. Mytheli Sreenivas, 'Sexuality and Modern Imperialism', in *A Global History of Sexuality: The Modern Era*, ed. Robert M. Buffington, Eithne Luibhéid, and Donna J. Guy, Hoboken: John Wiley & Sons, 2013, 60.

18. Mamdani, *Citizen and Subject*, 3.

19. Thomas Williamson quoted in Sreenivas, 'Sexuality', 62.

20. Ann L. Stoler, 'Making Empire Respectable: The Politics of Race and Sexual Morality in 20th-Century Colonial Cultures', *American Ethnologist* 16: 4, 1989, 639.

21. Kenneth Ballhatchet, *Race, Sex, and Class Under the Raj: Imperial Attitudes and Policies and Their Critics, 1793–1905*, India: St. Martin's Press, 1980, 83.

22. Chitty, *Sexual Hegemony*, 35.

23. Ronald Hyam, *Empire and Sexuality: The British Experience*, Manchester: Manchester University Press, 1990, 3.

24. See Ballhatchet, *Race, Sex, and Class Under the Raj*.

25. Parliamentary Papers, House of Commons, 197 (1888), 4 June 1888, quoted in Philippa Levine, 'Venereal Disease, Prostitution, and the Politics of Empire: The Case of British India'. *Journal of the History of Sexuality* 4: 4, 1994.

26. Levine, 'Venereal Disease', 599.

27. Vron Ware, *Beyond the Pale: White Women, Racism, and History*, London: Verso, 2015, 131.

28. Stoler, *Race and the Education of Desire*, 27.

29. Talwar Oldenburg, 'Lifestyle as Resistance: The Case of the Courtesans of Lucknow, India', *Feminist Studies* 16: 2, 1990, 260.

30. Levine, 'Venereal Disease', 595.

31. Robinson, *Forgeries of Memory*, xii.

32. Stoler, 'Making Empire Respectable', 634.

33. Mary Procida, ' "The Greater Part of My Life Has Been Spent in India": Autobiography and the Crisis of Empire in the Twentieth Century', *Biography* 2002, 145.

34. Ware, *Beyond the Pale*, 38.

35. Forster, 'The Other Boat', 193.

36. Ware, *Beyond the Pale*, 162.

37. Quoted in Ware, *Beyond the Pale*, 237.

38. Ibid., 40.

39. Quoted Smith and Marmo, *Race, Gender and the Body*, 85.

40. Levine, 'Venereal Disease', 593.

41. Ibid.

42. Hardy, quoted in Stoler, 'Making Empire Respectable', 648.

43. Forster, 'The Other Boat', 192.
44. Ibid., 174.
45. Ibid., 197.

## 4 National Family

1. Taylor quoted in David Edgerton, 'War and the Development of the British Welfare State', in *Warfare and Welfare: Military Conflict and Welfare State Development in Western Countries*, ed. Herbert Obinger, Klaus Petersen, and Peter Starke, Oxford: Oxford Academic, 2018, 213.
2. Edgerton, 213.
3. Anna Davin, 'Imperialism and Motherhood', *History Workshop* 5, 1978, 10.
4. Sir Frederick Maurice, *Sir Frederick Maurice; a Record of His Work and Opinions, with Eight Essays on Discipline and National Efficiency*, ed. Frederick Barton Maurice, London: E. Arnold, 1913, 118.
5. Foucault, *History of Sexuality*, 139.
6. Davin, 'Imperialism and Motherhood', 12.
7. Ibid., 16.
8. Goldberg, *The Racial State*, 104.
9. Partha Chatterjee, The Nation and its Fragments: Colonial and Postcolonial Histories, Princeton: Princeton University Press, 1993, 18.
10. Quoted in Patel, *We're Here Because You Were There*, 50.
11. C.V. Wedgwood, *The King's Peace*, Pennsylvania: Penn State University Press, 1983, 63.
12. George Orwell, 'The Lion and the Unicorn: Socialism and the English Genius', Orwell Foundation website.
13. Alastair Bonnett, 'How the British Working Class became White: The Symbolic (Re) Formation of Racialized Capitalism', *Journal of Historical Sociology* 11: 3, 1998.
14. Gail Lewis and Clare Hemmings, '"Where Might We Go If We Dare": Moving Beyond the "Thick, Suffocating Fog of Whiteness" in Feminism', *Feminist Theory* 20: 4, 2019.
15. Kerem Nişancıoğlu, Sita Balani, Kojo Koram, Gargi Bhattacharyya, Dalia Gebrial, Adam Elliott-Cooper, *Empire's Endgame: Racism and the British State*, London: Pluto Press, 2021, 106–7.

16. Selma James, 'The Family Allowance Campaign' in *Sex, Race and Class – The Perspective of Winning: A Selection of Writings 1952–2011*, Oakland: PM Press, 2012.

17. Sivamohan Valluvan, *The Clamour of Nationalism: Race and Nation in Twenty-First-Century Britain*, Manchester: Manchester University Press, 2019, 175.

18. Patel, *We're Here Because You Were There*, 4.

19. Ibid., 62–3.

20. Ibid., 1.

21. Nadine El-Enany, *(B)ordering Britain: Law, Race and Empire*, Manchester: Manchester University Press, 6.

22. Luke de Noronha, 'Indian Migration and Empire: Comment by Luke de Noronha', *The Disorder of Things*, 19 February 2021.

23. Rachel A. Hall, 'When is a Wife not a Wife? Some Observations on the Immigration Experiences of South Asian Women in West Yorkshire', *Contemporary Politics* 8: 1, 2002.

24. Smith and Marmo, *Race, Gender and the Body*, 52.

25. Helena Wray, 'Moulding the Migrant Family', *Legal Studies* 29: 4, 2009, 612.

26. Parita Trivedi, 'To Deny our Fullness: Asian Women in the Making of History', *Feminist Review* 17: 1, 1984, 46.

27. Pratibha Parmar, 'Gender, Race and Class: Asian Women in Resistance', in *Empire Strikes Back*, ed. Centre for Contemporary Cultural Studies, New York: Routledge, 2005, 245.

28. Rachel A. Hall, 60.

29. Radhika Mongia, *Indian Migration and Empire: A Colonial Genealogy of the Modern State*, Durham: Duke University Press, 2018, 110.

30. Bhattacharyya, *Crisis, Austerity, and Everyday Life*, 166.

31. Gail Lewis, 'Unsafe travel: Experiencing intersectionality and feminist displacements', Signs 28 no 4 (2013): 877.

32. Lowe, 'The Intimacies of Four Continents', 201.

33. Moynihan quoted in Cohen, 'Punks, Bulldaggers, and Welfare Queens', 436.

34. Adam Elliott-Cooper, *Black Resistance to British Policing*, Manchester: Manchester University Press, 2020, 100.

35. Luke de Noronha, *Deporting Black Britons: Portraits of Deportation to Jamaica*, Manchester: Manchester University Press, 2021, 26.

## 5  Divide and Assimilate

1. Seumas Milne, 'After the May Day Flood', *London Review of Books*, 5 June 1997.
2. Elizabeth Cohen quoted in Bridget Anderson, '"Heads I Win. Tails You Lose". Migration and the Worker Citizen', *Current Legal Problems* 68: 1, 2015, 191.
3. Anderson, '"Heads I Win. Tails You Lose"', 179-196, 191.
4. Quoted in Anderson, '"Heads I Win. Tails You Lose"', 187.
5. *The Sun*, 7 March 2001.
6. Natalie Edwards, 'Queer British Television: Policy and Practice, 1997-2007', PhD dissertation, University of Nottingham, 2010, 32.
7. Arun Kundnani, *The End of Tolerance: Racism in 21st Century Britain*, London: Pluto Press, 2007, 73.
8. Ibid., 74.
9. Quoted in Richard Seymour, *The Meaning of David Cameron*, London: Zer0 Books, 2010, 65.
10. James Meadway, 'Neoliberalism is Dying – Now We Must Replace It', *Open Democracy*, 3 September 2021.
11. Ibid.
12. Ben Miller, 'The Life and Death of Modern Homosexuality', *The Baffler*, 28 January 2021.
13. Seymour, *The Meaning of David Cameron*, 65.
14. Anthony Giddens, *The Transformation of Intimacy: Sexuality, Love, and Eroticism in Modern Societies*, Redwood City: Stanford University Press, 1992, 96.
15. Ibid., 2.
16. Ibid., 27.
17. Ibid., 61.
18. Ibid., 15.
19. Ibid., 28.
20. Ibid., 96.
21. Quoted in Jeffrey Weeks, *The World We Have Won: The Remaking of Erotic and Intimate Life*, Abingdon: Taylor & Francis, 2007, 192.
22. Edwards, 'Queer British Television', 76.
23. Stuart Hall, 'The Great Moving Nowhere Show', *Marxism Today* 1, 1998, 12.

24. Robbie Shilliam, 'Redeeming the "Ordinary Working Class"', *Current Sociology* 68: 2, 2020, 226.

25. *Supporting Families: A Consultation Document*, Great Britain: Home Office, 1998.

26. Karen Robson and Richard Berthoud, *Early Motherhood and Disadvantage: A Comparison between Ethnic Groups*, Institute for Social and Economic Research, ISER working paper, 2003, 5.

27. Ibid., 4.

28. See Anandi Ramamurthy, *Black Star*, London: Pluto Press, 2013, for an excellent account of the Asian Youth Movement.

29. Kundnani, 'From Oldham to Bradford: The Violence of the Violated', Institute of Race Relations, 1 October 2001.

30. Yasmin Hussain and Paul Bagguley, *Riotous Citizens: Ethnic Conflict in Multicultural Britain*, Abingdon: Taylor & Francis, 2016, 'Preface'.

31. Kundnani, 'From Oldham to Bradford'.

32. Bagguley and Hussain, chapter 2, 'The Criminalization of Pakistani and Bangladeshi Men'.

33. Nirpal Singh Dhaliwal, *Tourism*, London: Vintage, 2006, 151.

34. Jay Bernard and Sita Balani, 'Against Mastery: A Dialogue on Ta-Nehisi Coates's *The Water Dancer*', *The White Review*, July 2020.

35. Kundnani, *The End of Tolerance*, 52.

36. Angela McRobbie, *The Aftermath of Feminism*, London: Sage Publications Ltd, 2009, 70.

37. Ibid., 69.

38. Quoted in Amrit Wilson, *Dreams, Questions, Struggles*, London: Pluto Press, 2006, 87.

39. Lizzie Dearden, 'Suella Braverman says it is her 'dream' and 'obsession' to see a flight take asylum seekers to Rwanda', *Independent*, 5 October 2022.

## 6 Identity Crisis

1. Sarfraz Manzoor, *Greetings from Bury Park*, London: Bloomsbury, 2008.

2. Sathnam Sanghera, *The Boy With The Topknot/If You Don't Know Me By Now*, London: Penguin, 2008/2009.

3. Sathnam Sanghera, *Marriage Material*, London: Random House, 2013.

4. Esther Saxey, *Homoplot: The Coming-out Story and Gay, Lesbian and Bisexual Identity*, New York: Peter Lang, 2008, 3.

5. Sanghera, *The Boy With The Topknot*, 42.

6. Ibid., 298.

7. Quoted in Talal Asad, 'Multiculturalism and British Identity in the Wake of the Rushdie Affair', *Politics & Society* 18: 4, 1990, 457.

8. Asad, 'Multiculturalism', 457.

9. Ibid., 475.

10. Kundnani, 'From Oldham to Bradford'.

11. Barbara and Karen Fields, *Racecraft: The Soul of Inequality in American Life*, London: Verso Books, 2014, 76.

12. For more on conviviality, see Paul Gilroy, *After Empire*, New York: Routledge, 2004; Sivamohan Valluvan, 'Conviviality and Multiculture: A Post-Integration Sociology of Multi-Ethnic Interaction', *Young* 24: 3, 2016; Luke de Noronha, The Conviviality of the Overpoliced, Detained and Expelled: Refusing Race and Salvaging the Human at the Borders of Britain', *Sociological Review* 70: 1, 2022; Ben Rogaly, *Stories from a Migrant City*, Manchester: Manchester University Press, 2020.

13. Virinder Kalra, 'Between Emasculation and Hypermasculinity: Theorizing British South Asian Masculinities', *South Asian Popular Culture* 7: 2, 2009, 113.

14. Ibid., 113.

15. Ibid., 122.

16. Koushik Banarjea and Partha Banarjea, 'Psyche and Soul: A View from the South' in *Dis-Orienting Rhythms: The Politics of the New Asian Dance Music* ed. by Sanjay Sharma, John Hutnyk, and Ash Sharma, London: Zed Books, 1996, 113.

17. J. Strachey quoted in Kalra, 'Between Emasculation and Hypermasculinity', 121.

18. Mrinalini Sinha, *Colonial Masculinity: The 'Manly Englishman' and the 'Effeminate Bengali' In the Late Nineteenth Century*, Manchester: Manchester University Press, 1995, 17.

19. Kim Wagner, 'Thugs and Assassins', in *The Oxford Handbook of the History of Terrorism*, ed. Carola Dietze and Claudia Verhoeven, Oxford: Oxford University Press, 2021, 129.

20. Quoted in Wagner, 'Thugs and Assassins', 128.

21. Kalra, 'Between Emasculation and Hypermasculinity', 122–3.

22. Puar, *Terrorist Assemblages*, 196.

23. *My Brother the Devil*, directed by Sally El Hosaini, Rooks Nest Entertainment, 2012.

24. Quoted in Joseph Boone, 'Vacation Cruises; Or, The Homoerotics of Orientalism', *PMLA/Publications of the Modern Language Association of America* 110: 1, 1995, 92.

25. Claire Alexander, *The Asian Gang: Ethnicity, Identity, Masculinity*, Oxford: Berg, 2000, xiii.

26. Wendy Brown, *Regulating Aversion: Tolerance in the Age of Identity and Empire*, Princeton NJ: Princeton University Press, 2008, 151.

27. Stuart Hall, Chas Critcher, Tony Jefferson, John Clarke, and Brian Roberts, *Policing the Crisis: Mugging, the State and Law and Order*, London: Bloomsbury Publishing, 2017.

28. Dalia Gebrial, 'The Far Right Don't Care About Sexual Violence – They're Just Trying to Gain Political Power', *Novara Media*, 1 December 2018.

29. Bhattacharyya et al., *Empire's Endgame*, 115.

30. Banarjea and Banarjea, 'Psyche and Soul', 115.

31. Alexander, *The Asian Gang*, 5.

32. Arun Kundnani, 'Islamophobia: Lay Ideology of US-led Empire', www.kundnani.org, 2016, 3.

33. Bhattacharyya, *Dangerous Brown Men*, 35.

34. David Cameron, 'Muscular Liberalism' Speech, Munich Security Conference, Munich, 5 February 2011.

35. Azfar Shafi and Asim Qureshi, *Stranger than Fiction: How 'Pre-Crime' Approaches to 'Countering Violent Extremism' Institutionalise Islamophobia – A European Comparative Study*, The Transnational Institute, 11 February 2020, 8.

36. Rizwaan Sabir, 'Blurred Lines and False Dichotomies: Integrating Counterinsurgency into the UK's Domestic "War on Terror"', *Critical Social Policy* 37: 2, 2017, 206.

37. Dirks, *Castes of Mind*, 44.

38. Deanna Heath, 'Torture, the State, and Sexual Violence against Men in Colonial India', *Radical History Review* 2016: 126, 2016, 131.

39. Judith Butler, 'Sexual Politics, Torture, and Secular Time', *British Journal of Sociology* 59: 1, 2008, 16.

40. Ibid., 18.

41. Alex MacDonald, 'Gary McKinnon Has Asperger's Syndrome; So Does Talha Ahsan', *Huffington Post*, 16 December 2012.

## 7 Dangerous Brown Women

1. *Bodyguard*, directed by Thomas Vincent and John Strickland, 2018.
2. I borrow this phrase from Gargi Bhattacharyya's book *Dangerous Brown Men*.
3. Gayatri Chakravorty Spivak, 'Can the Subaltern Speak?' in *Colonial Discourse and Post-Colonial Theory*, ed. Patrick Williams and Laura Chrisman, New York: Routledge, 2015, 92.
4. John Ruskin, 'Sesame and Lilies', in *Sesame and Lilies*, New Haven: Yale University Press, 2008.
5. Naaz Rashid, *Veiled Threats: Representing the Muslim Woman in Public Policy*, Bristol: Policy Press, 2016.
6. Elliott-Cooper, 71.
7. Naaz Rashid, 'Just A Girl: Thinking Intersectionally about 'The Muslim Girl' and Writing against Culture', *YOUNG* 24: 3, 2016.
8. Kalpana Wilson, '"Race", Gender and Neoliberalism: Changing Visual Representations in Development', *Third World Quarterly* 32: 2, 2011.
9. Yahya Birt, 'Astroturfing and the Rise of the Secular Security State in Britain', Medium.com, 2019.
10. Lila Abu-Lughod, 'Do Muslim Women Really Need Saving? Anthropological Reflections on Cultural Relativism and its Others', *American Anthropologist* 104: 3, 2002, 788.
11. Frantz Fanon, *A Dying Colonialism*, trans Haakon Chevalier, New York: Grove/Atlantic, Inc., 1994, 37–8.
12. Meyda Yeğenoğlu, *Colonial Fantasies: Towards a Feminist Reading of Orientalism*, Cambridge: Cambridge University Press, 1998, 55.
13. Ibid., 40.
14. Ibid., 64.
15. Mary Ann Doane, quoted ibid., 65.
16. Jacqueline Rose, 'Margaret Thatcher and Ruth Ellis', *New Formations* 6: 3, 1988, 4.
17. Neha Shah, 'How Did British Indians Become So Prominent in the Conservative Party?' *The Guardian*, 27 February 2019.

18. Jacqueline Rose, *On Violence and On Violence Against Women*, London: Faber & Faber, 2021, 16.
19. Rose, 'Thatcher', 9.
20. Chitty, *Sexual Hegemony*, 188.

## 8  Think of the Children

1. Sophie Lewis, 'SERF 'n' TERF', *Salvage*, 6 February 2017.
2. Rahul Rao, 'The Locations of Homophobia', *London Review of International Law*. 2. 2014, 169–99, 170.
3. Rao, *Out of Time*, 143.
4. Puar, *Terrorist Assemblages*, xii.
5. Jenny Kitzinger, 'Who Are You Kidding? Children, Power and the Struggle Against Sexual Abuse', in *Constructing and Reconstructing Childhood: Contemporary Issues in the Sociological Study of Childhood*, ed. Alan Prout and Allison James, London: Routledge, 2015, 162.
6. Lee Edelman, *No Future*, Durham: Duke University Press, 2004, 11.
7. Kitzinger, 'Who Are You Kidding?', 158.
8. Carolyn Steedman, *Landscape for a Good Woman*, London: Virago, 2005, 136.
9. See Salma Haidrani, 'Five Queer British Muslims on the LGBTQ+ Lessons Row', *Vice*, 28 March 2019; Asifa Lahore, 'As a Queer Muslim, Birmingham's Anti-LGBT Rhetoric "Limits the Progress" We've Fought Hard For', *Gay Times*, 2019; Louis Staples, 'If You are Uncomfortable with Your Child Being Told About LGBT+ People, Then You Are Being Homophobic', *Independent*, 20 March 2019.
10. Abeera Khan, 'In Defence of an Unalienated Politic: A Critical Appraisal of the "No Outsiders" Protests', *Feminist Review* 128: 1, 2021, 142.
11. Jyoti Puri, *Sexual States: Governance and the Struggle Over the Anti-sodomy Law in India*, Durham: Duke University Press, 2016, 5.
12. David Cameron, "Extremism" Speech, Ninestiles School, Birmingham, 20 July 2015.
13. Samir Shackle, 'Trojan Horse: The Real Story Behind the Fake "Islamic Plot" To Take Over Schools', *The Guardian*, 1 September 2017.
14. John Holmwood and Therese O'Toole, *Countering Extremism in British Schools?: The Truth about the Birmingham Trojan Horse Affair*, London: Policy Press, 2018.

15. William Callison and Quinn Slobodian, 'Coronapolitics from the Reichstag to the Capitol', *Boston Review*, 12 January 2021.

16. For a sensitive discussion of these issues, see Deborah Grayson, and Tamanda Walker, 'Religion, the Secular and the Left', *Soundings* 73: 73, 2019.

17. See 'In Support of A Woman's Place and Free Speech', southallblacksisters. org.uk, 24 February 2020.

18. Sima Kotecha, 'Birmingham LGBT Lessons: Head Teacher Threatened', BBC, 20 May 2019.

19. Nosheen Iqbal, 'Birmingham School Row: "This is Made Out to be Just Muslims v Gays. It's not"', *The Guardian*, 21 September 2019.

20. Callison and Slobodian, 'Coronapolitics'.

21. Julia O'Connell Davidson, *Children in the Global Sex Trade*, London: Wiley, 2005, 2.

22. Ibid.

23. Richard Seymour, 'Ezekiel's Wheel: QAnon as a Conversion Machine', Patreon, 24 March 2021.

24. Lizzie Dearden, 'Darren Osborne: How Finsbury Park Terror Attacker Became 'Obsessed' with Muslims in Less than a Month', *Independent*, 2 February 2018.

## Coda: The promise that would never be kept

1. Dirks, *Castes of Mind*, 10.

2. Mies quoted in Bhattacharyya, *Crisis, Austerity and Everyday Life*, 169.

3. Fraser, 'Behind Marx's Hidden Abode'.

4. Richard Seymour, 'The Year of Prophetic Desire', *Salvage*, 22 September 2021.

5. Chitty, *Sexual Hegemony*, 176.

6. Jordy Rosenberg, 'The Daddy Dialectic', *Los Angeles Review of Books*, 11 March 2018.

# Index